"Selina Hastings, Countess of Huntingdon, was one of the most influential evangelical figures of the eighteenth century, yet she remains relatively unknown today. I am happy to recommend this sympathetic and informative spiritual biography of Hastings."

Thomas S. Kidd
Author, *George Whitefield: America's Spiritual Founding Father*

"When I took the standard seminary two-term survey of Church History (known as Church History I & II) at the Toronto School of Theology in the mid-1970s during my masters studies, the central role of women in the life of the church was not a prominent highlight. I suspect that this was typical of many such survey courses at that time. Thankfully, church historians today know better and have been seeking to remedy this lacuna in various types of historical and biographical studies. This new biography by Priscilla Wong of a central, though oft-neglected, figure of the revivals of the eighteenth century, Selina Hastings, is a good example of what is needed: accessible, yet grounded in solid research; sympathetic, yet without being hagiographical; and sensitive to the lessons that can be derived from the way that God worked through this notable woman's life."

Michael A.G. Haykin
Chair & professor of church history, The Southern Baptist Theological Seminary and Professor of church history, Heritage Seminary, Cambridge, Ontario.

"Priscilla Wong skillfully demonstrates why Selina Hastings, the Countess of Huntingdon was one of the most significant women of the eighteenth–century Evangelical Revival. This valuable introduction reveals the boldness and creativity of Lady Huntingdon's inspiring life and ministry."

Tom Schwanda
Associate professor, emeritus of Christian Formation and Ministry, Wheaton College

"It's almost impossible to read an account of eighteenth-century Christianity without encountering the name of Selina Hastings. While her greatest influence was in England, her desire to see the gospel spread to every nation brought her in contact with Christians in many continents. Many well-known preachers acknowledged a debt of gratitude to the countess for the extent of their ministry. And yet, today, her story is still not widely known. In this fascinating biography, Priscilla Wong explores primary sources to unveil many facets of the countess' life, helping readers to understand her faith, dreams, and challenges as a woman, wife, mother, friend, evangelist, church planter, and benefactor. Readers will form a close bond with this exceptional woman and be inspired to set their eyes on the same Christ that had captivated her life."

Simonetta Carr
Author, *Questions Women Asked* and the Christian Biographies for Young Readers series

The Bold Evangelist

THE BOLD EVANGELIST

The Life and Ministry of **Selina Hastings**,
Countess of Huntingdon

PRISCILLA WONG

The Bold Evangelist: The Life and Ministry of Selina Hastings, Countess of Huntingdon

Copyright © 2021 Priscilla Wong

All rights reserved. This book may not be reproduced, in whole or in part, without written permission from the publishers.

H&E Publishing, Peterborough, Ontario, Canada
www.hesedandemet.com

Cover design by Chance Faulkner
Interior font: Equity Text A
Cover Portrait by Marcos Rodrigues
Portrait colorization by Paul Cox, reftoons.com

Paperback ISBN: 978-1-77484-016-0
Hardcover ISBN: 978-1-77484-018-4
Ebook ISBN: 978-1-77484-017-7

To my husband Lee—
may the faithfulness
of Selina in her gospel ministry
spur us on in ours.

Contents

Timeline xi
Foreword xv
    Karen Swallow Prior
Introduction 1
1. Historical and Religious Landscape 7
2. Early Life and Marriage 13
3. Portrait of the Wife and Mother 21
4. Portrait of the Countess before Conversion 35
5. The Conversion of the Countess and Some Methodist Leaders ... 39
6. The Countess and the Early Methodist Revival 49
7. Divisions and Bonds 59
8. Shattering Losses 73
9. Drawing-Room Evangelism 79
10. The Countess' Chapels 87
11. Trevecca College 97
12. The Minutes Controversy 109
13. The Bethesda Orphan House 119
14. A Painful Separation 139
15. Lessons from the Life of Selina Hastings 149

Acknowledgements 157
About the Author 159
Suggested Further Reading 161
Subject Index 163
Scripture Index 167

Timeline

24 August 1707	Selina Hastings (née Shirley) born in Northhamptonshire
3 June 1728	Marries Theophilus Hastings, ninth Earl of Huntingdon
13 March 1729	Son Francis Hastings is born
29 March 1730	Son George Hastings is born
March 1731	Daughter Elizabeth Hastings is born
23 January 1732	Son Ferdinando Hastings is born
June 1735	Daughter Selina Hastings is born (dies in infancy)
3 December 1737	Daughter also named Selina Hastings is born
July 1739	Conversion takes place shortly after hearing the testimony of sister-in-law Lady Margaret Hastings
	Sister-in-law Lady Betty Hastings dies of cancer
12 December 1739	Last child Henry Hastings is born
1739/1740	John Wesley and George Whitefield dispute over the doctrine of Predestination

1740	John Wesley along with his supporters separates from the Moravians because of controversial "stillness" doctrine
	Friendship with John and Charles Wesley develop. Selina sides with the Wesleys on the predestination debate
November 1741	Lady Margaret Hastings marries Benjamin Ingham
	Selina supports John Wesley's doctrine of Christian Perfection
1743	Sons Ferdinando and George die of smallpox
13 October 1746	Husband Theophilus Hastings dies of a stroke
1747	Howell Harris' diary indicates Selina's rejection of perfection doctrine
1748	Appoints George Whitefield as her chaplain; her home becomes a place for "drawing-room evangelism"
	Shifts theologically, siding with Whitefield on predestination doctrine
September 1758	Youngest son Henry dies
1761	Sets up a chapel in the popular town of Brighton, partially funding the project by selling her jewels
1762	Sets up another chapel near Brighton, Ote Hall
12 May 1763	Youngest daughter Lady Selina dies

1765	Establishes the Bath Chapel
	Compiles a hymnbook of 231 hymns to be sung at all her chapels
24 August 1768	Opens Trevecca College in South Wales, a collaborative project with Howell Harris
1769	Establishes a chapel in Tunbridge Wells
August 1770	The Minutes Controversy erupts following John Wesley's London conference and the publication of his *Minutes*
30 September 1770	George Whitefield dies during his seventh trip to North America and leaves Selina his Bethesda Orphanage in Savannah, Georgia
December 1772	Sends a mission team to Georgia in hopes of establishing a college for ministerial training
1773	African-American poet Phillis Wheatley dedicates her book *Poems on Various Subjects, Religious and Moral* to Lady Huntingdon, her patroness
1775	War of American Independence causes Selina to lose contact with her Georgian mission team. (State of Georgia takes possession of her American estates upon her death.)
1779	Spa Fields Chapel in London opens
January 1782	After Selina's Spa Fields Chapel is prohibited from operating due to

	violation of parish boundaries, Selina decides to separate from the Church of England. The *Countess of Huntingdon's Connexion* is formed.
1789	Oldest son Francis dies (her oldest daughter Elizabeth dies in 1808)
17 June 1791	Dies at her London home

Foreword

"The Slave Trade was always unjustifiable; but inattention and interest prevented, for a time, the evil from being perceived."

These are the words of John Newton, quoted later in this book. With these words, Newton—Christian convert, former slave ship captain, and author of the beloved hymn, "Amazing Grace"—struggled to explain, years later, how a practice as depraved as slavery was one to which he could turn a blind eye for so long.

Newton wasn't alone, of course. Many Christians, including many of Christians who played key roles in the evangelical revivals that swept across England and America and beyond centuries ago, could not or would not see this great evil of their time. This paradox—helping usher in a spiritual awakening that would change the world while remaining asleep in the midst of a great moral and social crisis—serves as a parable of the church and of the human condition itself.

So, too, the life of Selina Hastings, Countess of Huntingdon, presents just such a paradox and just such a parable.

Newton's words above offer important insight into how even faithful, devoted, serious Christians—such as Hastings, but even more, such as countless believers in every time, every age, and in endless ways—can with one hand do so much good and with the other hand fail to do right. As Newton suggests, this failure often owes simply to not paying attention or to the ease with which we are prone to rationalizing wrong when it is in our personal interest to do so. Often, it is both. After all, we choose what we pay attention to, and that choice is often determined by self-interest.

And herein lies one of the good gifts offered by the study of the lives of others, and in particular, the lives of other Christians, whether past and present. The backdrop of other people's lives and their times has a way of placing right and wrong, strength and weakness, in stark relief. In the lives of others, it is easier to see more clearly those things that go beyond our own interests, to recognize the moral truths that transcend our own place and situation, and to take encouragement where encouragement might be needed and correction where that, too, ought to be taken.

In Selina Hastings, Countess of Huntingdon we find correction and great encouragement.

According to worldly ways of thinking, Hastings was an unlikely convert, let alone one who promised to be a "bold evangelist."

She disproved the pattern, first, by being an adult convert. Moreover, she converted within a nominally Christian culture, the sort that tends to be an inoculation against genuine Christian belief. Indeed, as detailed in the pages that follow, Hastings lived during a time and in a place of spiritual decline, where the record of Christian conversions was low. Yet, in God's providence, the revivals led by brothers John and Charles Wesley, along with those of George Whitefield, crossed paths with this spiritually hungry woman at just the right time in her life—and just the right time in history, too.

Unlike the majority of those brought to faith by the early evangelical movement, who tended to be from the masses of the poor and working class, Hastings was a member of the nobility. Indeed, she was one from among those of whom Jesus said it would be easier for a camel to go through the eye of a needle than for them to enter the kingdom of heaven. Yet, this noblewoman aligned herself, not only with Christ, but with the rabble-rousing, low church evangelicals whose revivalist, enthusiastic ways were largely rejected by both high society and the established church. Through Hastings, this new movement of the Spirit met old wealth and old traditions, wedging open new opportunities for the advancement of Christian teaching and living. Hastings stewarded her wealth, her homes, her connections, and her time—all of her resources—not only to spreading the gospel herself, but to equipping and empowering others to do the same.

Through it all, Hastings experienced personal, familial, and theological struggles, as most of us do. Furthermore, upon her conversion, she entered a Christian culture which would become deeply divided doctrinally, politically, and socially, as our Christian culture is today. While some choose to reform flawed institutions from without, she strove (rightly or wrongly) to reform the institution of slavery from within. Most of us today face parallel dilemmas to reform from within or without.

Hastings was flawed (as are all earthly saints). We can see in her life weaknesses of both personality and moral imagination. The latter, especially, is not to be excused, but, rather, set forth as an example for us to learn from as we strive to see our own failures in ourselves and in the church in our time. Conscripted into the prevailing views of her time, she couldn't see beyond her finite world to the transcendent truths about human equality and dignity. We are no different.

We are also no different in the sense that we, too, can and should be bold evangelists as Hastings was, using all our

The Bold Evangelist

resources in our own lives and in our own times for the advancement of the gospel.

Karen Swallow Prior
July 2021

Introduction

If the reader is unacquainted with Selina Hastings, the Countess of Huntingdon (1707-1791), a starting point might be to recall the conversion of Lydia in the book of Acts, which describes her as the first convert in Europe during the apostle Paul's second missionary journey:

> And on the Sabbath day we went outside the gate to the riverside, where we supposed there was a place of prayer, and we sat down and spoke to the women who had come together. One who heard us was a woman named Lydia, from the city of Thyatira, a seller of purple goods, who was a worshiper of God. The Lord opened her heart to pay attention to what was said by Paul. And after she was baptized, and her household as well, she urged us, saying, "If you have judged me to be faithful to the Lord, come to my house and stay." And she prevailed upon us (Acts 16:13-15).

Lydia was among a group of women who were praying by the riverside on the Sabbath. She was originally from the city of Thyatira in Asia Minor but happened to be doing business in Europe. The purple goods that she sold included Tyrian purple dye, a scarce and valuable commodity. This and also the fact that she owned multiple homes indicate her affluence and privileged position. Materially Lydia was fulfilled, but the above portrait reveals her desire for spiritual fulfillment.

Upon hearing the gospel message, Lydia was converted. But the narrative does not end there. She was eager to share the good news with her entire household, who were converted as a result of her testimony. Afterwards she extended a firm and welcome invitation to Paul and his friends to stay at her home, and as a result of her hospitality, Lydia's home became the setting for the first church in Europe, from which the gospel message spread throughout the continent.

Selina Hastings, the Countess of Huntingdon, played a significant role in the eighteenth-century Evangelical Revival, a period that began when some individuals, following their own conversions, became powerful agents in spreading the gospel message in Europe. The names George Whitefield (1714–1770) and John Wesley (1703–1791) are likely familiar to us, while Selina Hastings and her part in the Revival may be less known. Like Lydia, Selina was a woman of considerable wealth. As the wife of an Earl, she owned and managed many estates throughout Britain. Yet despite her riches and high position in society, she was not satisfied—she longed for real spiritual union with God. Exposed to the heartfelt preaching of the gospel during the Revival, she was converted in 1739 at the age of thirty-two. From this point forward the Countess devoted herself to a number of evangelistic causes, and like Lydia, provided settings where people could hear the gospel when circumstances would not normally have permitted it.

Selina's bold and persistent actions during the Revival cannot be understated. By the end of her life, with all of her resources, her many achievements included the establishment of over sixty chapels, a college for the training of ministers, and the denomination *Countess of Huntingdon's Connexion*. It has been said that the Countess' financial contribution to the Revival was over 12,000,000 pounds![1]

"A mother of Israel," Whitefield and others called her.[2] Further words from her trusted friends give us a sense of the impact Selina's Christian faith had on those around her:

---

[1] Douglas Bond, *Augustus Toplady* (Darlington: EP Books, 2012), 45.
[2] John R. Tyson with Boyd S. Schlenther, *In the Midst of Early Methodism: Lady Huntingdon and Her Correspondence* (Maryland: Scarecrow Press, 2006), 75, Letter from George Whitefield to Countess Delitz, October 11, 1750.

Introduction

From hymn-writer and nonconformist minister Philip Doddridge (1702-1751):

> The strength of her soul is amazing. I think I never saw so much of the image of God in a woman upon earth. Were I to write what I know of her, it would fill your heart with wonder, joy and praise. ... She has God dwelling in her and she is ever bearing her testimony to the present salvation he has given us, and to the foundation of waters which she feels springing up in her soul.[3]

From evangelical Anglican minister Henry Venn (1725-1797) who preached for the Countess at her chapels alongside many others:

> In Lady Huntingdon I see a star of the first magnitude in the firmament of the church ... No equipage—no livery—no house—all these given up that perishing sinners may hear the life-giving sound and be enriched with all spiritual blessings. Her prayers are heard, her chapel is crowded, and many sinners amongst the poor are brought into the City of Refuge. I feel from Lady Huntingdon's example an increasing desire both for myself and for you and all our friends that we may be active and eminent in the life of grace.[4]

Of course, as in any account of a human agent used by God, Selina was not without flaw or error. Biographical accounts reveal that she had a temper, and in some heated situations this was seen to flare up in her exchanges with others. Living in the upper crust of society, the Countess could sometimes be found to act imperiously toward her attendants, an attitude that would be met with criticism today. Encountering such, we must bear in mind what

---

[3] Faith Cook, *Selina Countess of Huntingdon: Her Pivotal Role in the 18th Century Evangelical Awakening* (Edinburgh: The Banner of Truth Trust, 2001), 134.
[4] Cook, *Countess of Huntingdon*, 269.

was considered characteristic of her time when distinct class structures were embedded; it was not so straightforward to simply step outside of the prevailing culture.[5] In some of Selina's ventures, individuals approached her and gave her advice, but when the Countess had committed herself to carrying out a course of action, she could be found unwilling to yield to counsel and deemed to be acting too rashly. But as we shall see, by the grace of God, filled with the Holy Spirit, Selina's desire and commitment to reach unsaved souls outshined the above.

We cannot help but be amazed by her productivity. She once wrote of her fear of spiritual idleness: "I dread slack hands in the vineyard; we must all up and be doing."[6] In the twenty-first century, an age of distraction and much preoccupation with producing material rewards but minimal of the spiritual, the Countess' tenacity is inspiring—from her conversion to the end of her life in realizing a vision that would see the gospel spread throughout the nations.

All the luxuries that came with one in Selina's station did not captivate her more than Christ did. Indeed she could have dressed as exquisitely as her female counterparts, but more and more she chose not to, as she expressed to a friend: "I see so much vanity of the great and rich that I long often to sink down to poverty, but the Lord holds mine eyes that they behold not vanity with any desire after it."[7] At one time she had even sold off her jewelry to fund the building of a chapel. Selina was willing to sacrifice personal extravagances to further the evangelistic cause.

At the same time, her shortcomings and the suffering she endured as a wife and mother enable us to connect with her even more deeply. Her ill health, the loss of her husband when she was

---

[5] Cook, *Countess of Huntingdon*, 16.

[6] Cook, *Countess of Huntingdon*, 101.

[7] Tyson, *Lady Huntingdon and Her Correspondence*, 59, Letter to Charles Wesley, June 29, 1742.

Introduction

still quite young, the death of her children (only one of her seven children survived her), the persecution she faced as a believer amid a parochial upper class—here we witness an individual, disheartened at times by trial, ready to give up, but by the Spirit's power, resolved to tread on.

Selina's example serves as great encouragement when it comes to our own spiritual journeys and what God has called each one of us to do. That temptation to cling to earthly comforts; that inclination to set modest goals, ones that rely on merely our own reason and resources; that friend, that neighbor, that stranger, the one we have been too afraid to approach with the truth of the gospel—may the life and ministry of Selina Hastings inspire us to go forward, as she had, with her eyes set not on this kingdom but the One to come.

1
Historical and Religious Landscape

No history is an isolated event but remains part of a greater narrative. The Evangelical Revival emerged during a time of spiritual drought in England. Selina Hastings was born here in the early part of the eighteenth century, and by this time, the fruit born by the revival movement of the sixteenth and seventeenth centuries had faded. A hundred years earlier was the Puritan movement, comprising a body of preachers and laymen who had sought to *purify* and reform the Church of England, which they considered to still possess traces of Roman Catholic religious practice that had no biblical basis in the life of the church.

This conviction, of course, had been the cry of the Reformation, which began in 1517, the year Martin Luther (1483–1546) formally protested against the Roman Catholic Church for the error of its ways. His *95 Theses*, nailed to the church door at Wittenberg in Germany, criticized the Roman Church's teachings and practices, which focused more on the work and merits of man. Salvation was not by the grace of God but through the church's administration of sacraments and dispensing of grace. Just as the danger of false teachings had threatened to creep into the Christian church in New Testament times, so it did in the ensuing centuries. The grave error had steered people away from the true gospel—that believers were delivered from their sins by the finished work of God in sacrificing his Son on the cross. No human effort could earn salvation. This was solely by the all-sufficient grace of God in saving the sinner.

While the effects of the Reformation had spread through Europe, it was least successful in taking root in England. The Puritans were the individuals who desired to finish the work that the

The Bold Evangelist

Reformation had begun. They were biblically-convicted that religious life within the state church needed to be radically transformed to reflect the model of the New Testament church. For the Puritans, this meant reviving Christian faith and practice within the church itself. Through the essential gospel truths preached by the pastors and genuine conversions and growth of the people, there was hope of impacting the state church, and thereupon, the nation.

The Puritans began operating under Queen Elizabeth's reign (1558-1603), and because she opposed their religious position, the Puritans faced harsh persecution. In the face of these trials, however, the Puritans grew even more strong and steadfast in their mission. When the English Civil War broke out in 1642, Oliver Cromwell (1599-1658) and his army fought for Parliament in the name of religious freedom. Cromwell, a Puritan, contested the idea of a specific form of church government and worship being imposed on the people. When Cromwell defeated the King's forces in 1645, he was appointed Lord Protector of England, thereby replacing the English monarchy. During the time that Cromwell was in power, changes were made to the state church, and people lived with a measure of religious liberty. When Cromwell died, support for his convictions on religious toleration waned, and in 1660, the monarchy was restored.

With the return of Charles II as king (1660-1685), the monarchy was once again committed to subverting the Puritans. As a result, with the Restoration came the loss of any prospect of reforming the nation. In due course, the Puritans, unwilling to submit to the demands of the state church, were left with no choice but to leave. The Great Ejection of 1662 saw 2000 ministers forced out of the Church of England. Those who worshipped outside of the state church from this point forward were considered "dissenters" or "nonconformists."

Historical and Religious Landscape

England would subsequently plunge into deep spiritual decline. Describing the spiritual state of eighteenth-century England, the great hymn-writer Isaac Watts (1674–1748) had described it as "the decay of vital religion in the hearts and lives of men."[1] There was little evidence of real conversions within the state church. Religious life was reduced to mere moralism and duty. Church life fixated on ritual and form. These practices led to Deism, a religion characterized by moral living but a distant, inaccessible God.

With the emergence of the Enlightenment in the same period, human reason began to take over. Science, philosophy, and rationalism became the focus. In other words, man was at the heart of things, not God. Enlightenment thinking also infiltrated the church where sermons became long and tedious explanations of theological concepts. From a religious perspective, human reason by itself did little for the soul. Absent from this was the mystery, beauty, and saving reality of the atoning sacrifice of God's Son on the cross. The message coming from the pulpit lacked any sort of divine power to move the sinner in the pew.

In this dry and weary land was a latent thirst for living water.

But zeal parallel to those of the first Reformers and Puritans emerged in the Evangelical Revival hundreds of years later. Like the movements before it, the Revival was a proclamation of God's grace—fully effective in saving the sinner—and the genuinely converted could anticipate and witness God's transforming work in their life. Selina Hastings, converted early on in the Revival, came to play a vital part in it, having ties with many of its key players, including John and Charles Wesley, George Whitefield, Benjamin Ingham, William Romaine, John Fletcher, John Berridge,

---

[1] Tim Dowley, *Introduction to The History of Christianity* (Minneapolis: Fortress Press, 2002), 447.

and Howell Harris. In fact, she was referred to by one historian as "the glue that held the Revival together."[2]

The Revival had commenced with the purpose of reforming the Church of England from within. George Whitefield, John Wesley, and Charles Wesley were all Anglican ministers. Initially they hung on to the hope that England would one day worship God as a nation, in one accord. But as much as they desired to operate within the state church, their message was seldom welcomed by the Anglican clergy, thus giving rise to the Methodist movement.

Methodism in the eighteenth century did not begin as a denomination as it is understood today. Rather it referred to those individuals who were recognized to be genuinely converted.[3] Many of the leaders continued to observe the Church of England's Thirty-Nine Articles, prayer book, and liturgy; however, their Methodist convictions led them to focus more on furthering itinerant preaching and establishing local societies for the spiritual nurturing of believers and less on adhering to Anglican tradition. The emphasis was on the internal transformation of the believer's life through the work of the Holy Spirit, not solely the external observation of religious rituals.

It was the gripping and forthright testimonies of preachers such as Whitefield and the Wesley brothers that raised the ears and moved the hearts of their hearers. And, indeed, there were thirsty souls: at one time, as many as thirty thousand people flocked to listen to the preaching of Whitefield. It was the Countess of Huntingdon that acted swiftly and resolutely to open up more venues for this preaching to take place. There were many who contributed to the Evangelical Revival; as a Countess and

---

[2] Richard Turnbull, *Reviving the Heart: The Story of the 18th Century Revival* (Oxford: Lion Hudson, 2012), 105.

[3] Edwin Welch, *Spiritual Pilgrim, A Reassessment of the Life of the Countess of Huntingdon* (Cardiff: University of Wales Press, 1995), 37.

Historical and Religious Landscape

peeress of the realm, Selina Hastings had her unique part, possessing not only means but influence, and it is to this part of the narrative with which we shall begin.

2
Early Life and Marriage

Much of this biography recounts the events following Selina Hastings' conversion, in part because her gospel ministry during those latter years is so remarkable, and also because most of her correspondence reveals what transpired during that period. The same cannot be said of her early life. Selina kept no journals or diaries that allow us to look intimately into her private existence. Historical records merely offer glimpses. Yet they nonetheless provide a clue to the woman we later meet. What of her past shaped her habits, character, and goals, and paved the way for the impressive work that lay ahead?

Selina Hastings (née Shirley) was born on 24 August 1707 at the Astwell Manor House in Northhamptonshire. The structure still stands today, though a farm has replaced the once distinguished home.[1] In keeping with tradition, it is likely that Selina was christened at the parish church, although no baptismal records survive.[2] The virtual silence of her first seventeen years is likely attributed to the discord that wrought the Shirley family prior to and during Selina's life, much of it stemming from battles over rights to the family assets.[3]

Royal Connections

Selina's ancestry can be traced back to royalty. In 1615 Sir Henry Shirley (Selina's great, great-grandfather, 1588-1633) married Dorothy Devereux, who was the daughter of Robert Devereux, the Earl of Essex. Robert Devereux's family descended directly

---

[1] Cook, *Countess of Huntingdon*, 1.
[2] Cook, *Countess of Huntingdon*, 6-7.
[3] Cook, *Countess of Huntingdon*, 1.

The Bold Evangelist

from King Edward III and IV.[4] Sir Henry Shirley's grandson, Sir Robert Shirley (Selina's grandfather, 1650–1717), was a loyal supporter of Charles II following the Restoration, and not long after, was granted the title Baron of Ferrers. However, he abandoned his loyalty when James II (brother of Charles II), a staunch Catholic, ascended the throne. Sir Robert's loyalty shifted to James II's youngest Protestant daughter, Princess Anne; his loyalty went as far as requesting the princess to be godmother to his youngest daughter. When Anne ascended the throne in 1702, the favor he earned in the Queen's sight helped him gain the titles of First Earl Ferrers and Viscount Tamworth.[5]

Sir Robert Shirley came to own a multitude of estates throughout England. His primary residences included Staunton Harold in Leicestershire and Chartley in Staffordshire as well as their surrounding property. In addition, he occupied homes or land in Derbyshire, Nottinghamshire, Warwickshire, Northhamptonshire (where Selina was born), and Wiltshire.[6]

Quarrels over the Shirley Wealth

Selina's father Washington Shirley (1677–1729) came into conflict with his father Robert regarding his entitlement to this wealth. The conflict emerged from the fact that Robert had in 1671 married Elizabeth Washington (1656–1693), a woman who also came from a reputable family, but who died at the age of 37; six years later, upon remarrying a woman named Selina Finch (1681–1762), he sought to cut off his assets from his first wife and her children.[7] The reason for this is not clear. The properties that had been passed down to Selina's grandfather were substantial. His fortune would have been more than adequate to support the children from

---

[4] Cook, *Countess of Huntingdon*, 1–2.
[5] Cook, *Countess of Huntingdon*, 2–3.
[6] Cook, *Countess of Huntingdon*, 3.
[7] Cook, *Countess of Huntingdon*, 3–4.

Early Life and Marriage

both his marriages.[8] Washington Shirley was the second son from Robert's first marriage. His father's callous actions would permanently sour his relations with Washington and his siblings.[9]

In 1704 Washington Shirley married Mary Levinge and they had three daughters: the eldest daughter Elizabeth was born around 1704; Selina (the subject of this biography) was next in 1707; and Mary in 1712. The fact that the Shirley family records have no log of the marriage date or the children's birth dates reveals the intense friction between Washington and his father.[10] The intentional naming of his eldest daughters hints to Washington's attempt at reconciliation, but sadly no peaceful outcome came of it.[11] He would discover upon his father's death in 1717 that the only item left to him in his father's will was the title of Second Earl of Ferrers. Disconcerting (and telling) is that among the fifty mourners at Robert Shirley's funeral, none of them were his children.[12]

What followed in those ensuing years were Washington's ongoing legal battles for what he believed was the right to his own inheritance being the eldest surviving son in the Shirley family. Washington would eventually succeed in safeguarding a portion of this inheritance for his family, but not without the agonies of countless lawsuits and family conflicts. These did not end with the settlement but persisted long after Washington's death. His children continued to face lawsuits from their other family members, and none of this was completely settled until twenty years after Selina's death.[13]

---

[8] Welch, *Spiritual Pilgrim*, 8.
[9] Welch, *Spiritual Pilgrim*, 8.
[10] Welch, *Spiritual Pilgrim*, 10.
[11] Cook, *Countess of Huntingdon*, 5.
[12] Welch, *Spiritual Pilgrim*, 12.
[13] Welch, *Spiritual Pilgrim*, 13.

A Turbulent Childhood

The strain between father and grandfather would have caused much distress for young Selina who was ten-years-old when her grandfather died. Even later in life, when much more was chronicled through her voluminous letters, she made almost no reference to these early years. With family circumstances already plagued by conflict, they were worsened still by the separation of her parents. Selina was only six-years-old. Marital breakdown had resulted from disputes over money and allegedly her mother's bitterness over Washington's extramarital affairs.[14] Selina's mother left with her younger sister Mary, spending the remainder of her life abroad in Europe. Selina and her older sister Elizabeth stayed with their father in Britain (Elizabeth passed away in 1734). Letters between Selina and her father reveal their close relationship, her father calling her "Linny" and "my dear" while her mother formally addressed her as "Madam."[15]

When Washington died in 1729 at the age of fifty-two, Selina's mother tried to gain rights to the family estates; when Selina herself acted against this, her mother reacted defiantly, resolving to disown her. Upon her mother's death a decade later, however, Selina acted sympathetically. Her mother had died with little to her name and so could not even finance the legacies she had wanted to leave behind. Selina paid for these legacies, for which her younger sister Mary, in a letter written in 1740, expressed her deep gratitude.[16]

From Turbulence to Peace

Selina's royal connections were also owing to her marriage to Theophilus Hastings (1696–1746), the ninth Earl of Huntingdon, and whose father was the seventh Earl of Huntingdon. As the

---

[14] Cook, *Countess of Huntingdon*, 7–8.
[15] Welch, *Spiritual Pilgrim*, 15.
[16] Cook, *Countess of Huntingdon*, 46–47.

Early Life and Marriage

eldest son of his father Theophilus Hastings' (1650-1701) second marriage, he was bequeathed the title when he was only eight-years-old upon the death of his half-brother George Hastings (1677-1704).[17] Theophilus' standing in court was so highly regarded that upon the coronation of King George II in 1727, the Earl had the distinction of carrying the Sword of State.[18]

Like the Shirley family, the Hastings family was wealthy, and even more so, with estates in Leicestershire and Derbyshire as well as properties in Loughborough, Ashby-de-la-Zouch, Ashby, Castle Donington (and nearby Donington Park), Leicester, Cambridge, and Huntingdon.[19] It was therefore important for the Hastings family to find like suitors, and in Selina they expressed their approval.[20] The two families were living nearby each other, the Shirleys at Staunton Harold (a property which Washington seized in 1724) and the Hastings at Donington Park.[21] Theophilus had one brother, Ferdinando, and four sisters, Anne (b. 1755), Frances (1694-1751), Catherine (1697-1740), and Margaret (1700-1768). Washington spent time with the Hastings hunting while warm friendships developed between Selina and Theophilus' sisters.[22]

Since Theophilus' father had died in 1701 and three years later his mother Frances had married a French prisoner of war that caused her to lose guardianship of the children, Theophilus and his siblings were looked after by relatives at different times; but Elizabeth Hastings (1682-1739), Theophilus' half-sister, whom they called Lady Betty, took upon herself the role of caregiver. She was the one who made arrangements for Theophilus to attend Christ Church in Oxford where the future Bishop of Gloucester

---

[17] Cook, *Countess of Huntingdon*, 11-12.
[18] Cook, *Countess of Huntingdon*, 16.
[19] Welch, *Spiritual Pilgrim*, 18.
[20] Cook, *Countess of Huntingdon*, 13.
[21] Cook, *Countess of Huntingdon*, 14.
[22] Welch, *Spiritual Pilgrim*, 20.

The Bold Evangelist

Martin Benson became his tutor and later his friend.[23] In time Lady Betty began to manage marriage prospects for her half-brother and it is in a letter from her to Theophilus that Selina is first mentioned in historical documents. The letter alludes to the intent of Theophilus' sisters to acquaint him with Selina.[24]

While arranged marriages were typical for those in their class, Selina and Theophilus' marriage was a genuinely loving one, evidenced in their letters. The dowry for the marriage was substantial: 15,000 pounds.[25] Selina's father took great measures to procure it, left with little option but to mortgage some of his estates since the family's ongoing legal battles had crippled him financially[26] (at the time of Selina's birth, Washington was working as a soldier at an army base in Ireland for scant pay[27]). But finally, on 3 June 1728, four years after their initial meeting, Selina and Theophilus were married in the church at Staunton Harold. Selina was twenty and Theophilus thirty-two. Donington Park became their first home together.[28] It was a joyful union, not just for the couple but the families. Having grown up in a household dominated by discord, Selina would have appreciated and even relished in the warm and tender home that eagerly welcomed her.

The Earl and Countess of Huntingdon

Lord and Lady Huntingdon were among the British ruling elite, representative of a very small but powerful group in Britain. As a peer of the realm, Lord Huntingdon was entitled to a seat in the upper house of Parliament known as the House of Lords. Though not permitted a seat, Selina as peeress had access to other privileges associated with the aristocratic title. Her privileges as

---

[23] Cook, *Countess of Huntingdon*, 12–13.
[24] Cook, *Countess of Huntingdon*, 13.
[25] Cook, *Countess of Huntingdon*, 14.
[26] Welch, *Spiritual Pilgrim*, 21.
[27] Cook, *Countess of Huntingdon*, 4.
[28] Cook, *Countess of Huntingdon*, 15.

Early Life and Marriage

peeress would become vital in the mid-1700s when she began building chapels throughout England. Even early on, however, the Countess was exerting her influence in the public sphere. On one occasion in 1739, displeased with being locked out from a particularly controversial debate in the gallery of the House of Lords, she along with a number of other noble ladies strategically stood outside from morning until evening creating a disturbance in hopes to gain entry. When this failed, the ladies deliberately fell silent, which successfully fooled authorities into believing the women had given up and left—but as soon as the doors crept open, the women swooped in to take their seats.[29]

Like others in their social rank, the Earl and Countess resided in their multiple lavish estates at different times throughout the year, whether in the bustling capital or the tranquil countryside. Their status also meant they were part of a prestigious circle of friends and acquaintances, and they naturally spent a great deal of their time socializing with royalty and other reputable men and women belonging to all spheres of influence. The couple attracted attention and merited respect. The Countess' movements and fashionable ensembles were sometimes the subject of gossip in letters of the nobility.[30] Following her conversion, Lady Huntingdon would use her standing with them to her advantage. Selina Hastings' distinct position of influence and wealth would serve a grand purpose in God's plan for the Revival in England.

---

[29] Cook, *Countess of Huntingdon*, 32–33.
[30] Cook, *Countess of Huntingdon*, 25, 32.

3
Portrait of the Wife and Mother

In a family portrait painted around 1744, Lord and Lady Huntingdon pose with their two youngest children, Selina, who is about seven, and Henry, who is about five. The Countess wears a dark elegant gown that sweeps to the ground, beautiful sheer fabric dressing her bodice, a string of pearls subtle against her fair skin. Little Henry's smile is most pronounced, his hand clasped in his mother's so that the Countess exemplifies both the tender mother and the genteel lady of her class. Daughter stands a distance away, her posture modeling courtesy and grace. Lord Huntingdon's arm stretches over, resting slightly on the Countess' shoulder, his patriarchal presence not overly dominant, which might actually reflect his relationship with his wife.

In tracing the Countess' steps in the Evangelical Revival, we might be so captivated by her later activity to the neglect of her earlier role as wife and mother. Selina cared deeply for her family and a glimpse into these family interactions uncovers a poignant picture of a woman who very much treasured the intimate moments spent with those nearest and dearest to her.

Love Letters of a Doting Wife
Even before Selina met Theophilus, she had been contemplating her prospects for marriage as other ladies naturally would have. A childhood overshadowed by wrangles between her parents and an early innocence stricken by their split had intensified her desire for a loving and long-lasting marriage. One of her biographers Thomas Haweis (1734–1820), who worked closely with her in her gospel ministry, recounted that this youthful yearning became one

of her earnest prayers.[1] The "serious" union that she had hoped for, one reflecting true depth and delight, would be fulfilled, attested by the many letters Selina wrote to her husband.

These letters coming into our hands can be credited to the many occasions when the couple was separated. Selina's ill health was the primary reason for this. Less than three and a half years after their wedding nuptials, Selina had given birth to four of her seven children and the childbearing had taken a toll on her body. In eighteenth-century England, the remedy was the waters of Bath. It was believed that the springs there had healing agents and their medicinal properties could relieve those who drank from and bathed in them.[2] Much against her will, Selina was urged to travel there, miles away from her husband and four young children. Selina took every opportunity to write to Theophilus. She called him "My Life" and "My Jewel" (and hence her children her "lives" and her "jewels"). She wrote frequently, never hesitating to express how profoundly she pined for his presence. Her friends in Bath could testify to her misery without him.[3] Her wifely affections are witnessed in a letter dated 19 February 1732:

> I find myself the most lost creature living and numberless sighs and tears upon the reflection of his absence daily about him, and I am quite resolved not even health itself another time shall part me from what I hold most dear on this side of the grave.
>
> I ever loved you to an excess of passion but since my absence from you I have felt greater pains than I ever thought that capable of giving and I hope in God I shall return to my dearest of Lives by the first week in April.[4]

---

[1] Cook, *Countess of Huntingdon*, 14.
[2] Cook, *Countess of Huntingdon*, 20-21.
[3] Tyson, *Lady Huntingdon and Her Correspondence*, 28, Letter from Selina to Theophilus, April 29, 1732.
[4] Tyson, *Lady Huntingdon and Her Correspondence*, 24.

Portrait of the Wife and Mother

The fact that Theophilus possessed an aversion to writing yet faithfully replied to his wife's letters confirms that the affections were mutual. Selina expressed her appreciation for the Earl's efforts:

> Saturday Post brought me my Dearest Lordship's most tender and affectionate Letter which almost overcame me with Joy to find my absence from you had not rendered me less fortunate in that esteem which is more valuable than any satisfaction I have on earth ... I know that writing to be a great Punishment to you.[5]

These love letters would also contain declarations of fidelity and commitment. While Bath was known for its therapeutic springs, it was also known for its shallowness and decadence. Sexual immorality was not unusual among her aristocratic peers and affairs were shamelessly exposed. Frequently were such reassurances from Selina to her husband:

> 14 February 1731:
> ... I may affirm that every succeeding day but increase that true fidelity and unshaken passion for [you] which nothing but being totally deprived [of your presence] can alter. And to enhance the former instant of my dearest Life's goodness. I had this day a valuable addition to it by another letter from you and that there is no pleasure to me equal.[6]

> 13 March 1732:
> ... I only wish to live to convince you of the sincerity of a heart that is so inviolably yours and that no time or circumstance of life can ever make less so.[7]

---

[5] Welch, *Spiritual Pilgrim*, 23.
[6] Tyson, *Lady Huntingdon and Her Correspondence*, 23.
[7] Tyson, *Lady Huntingdon and Her Correspondence*, 26.

The Bold Evangelist

Selina knew that rooted deeply in her husband's love for her was an instinct to protect her. Temporarily cut off from the family, she feared that this protection would go as far as keeping from her any news that would cause her heartache; so in a number of letters she pleads with Lord Huntingdon not to hold back anything critical regarding him or the children. A letter dated 16 February 1731 expresses her insistence on promptly returning should a serious incident arise:

> For as I have often assured my dearest Jewel that a share in his esteem is the bound of all my joys here on earth so he must believe those constant testimonies he gives me of it makes me of all creatures most happy, and petition as the greatest instance you can give me of it that if my dearest Life should be the least ill or any of my dear little ones, it may not be concealed from me, for I will that moment any night or day return to you.[8]

Anguished as Selina was by the painful separation, she did believe that it helped her to cherish her family all the more and could therefore voice her thankfulness during such trying circumstances:

> 30 March 1732:
> But I trust in that great and good God that He will soon restore me to those blessings [her family] He has once given and which he has in so remarkable a manner distinguished me in for the pain [of separation] that must attend the purpose of learning all I hold most dear would be inseparable.[9]

---

[8] Tyson, *Lady Huntingdon and Her Correspondence*, 24.
[9] Tyson, *Lady Huntingdon and Her Correspondence*, 27.

Portrait of the Wife and Mother

A Busy Household

Between the years of 1729 and 1739 Selina bore seven children. The day 13 March 1729 marked the birth of her first son Francis. Selina's father Washington Shirley was too ill to attend the christening and passed away a month after his grandson's birth. Selina's second son George was born a year later on 29 March 1730. A daughter whom they named Elizabeth was also born in March a year later. On 23 January 1732 her son Ferdinando was born. In June 1735, Selina, the fifth child, was born, although tragically she died in infancy. On 3 December 1737, another daughter was born, whom they also named Selina. Henry, the last child, was born on 12 December 1739.

Much of these early years were dedicated to tending to the responsibilities of caring for her husband and children. Selina also had the added stress of looking after the family estates, which she partially assumed upon her marriage and then fully after her husband's death. The Countess' strengths in organization and financial management were apparent in her meticulous and efficient ways of handling household affairs, including adding building extensions to existing properties, deciding on the architecture and décor of the homes, and collecting rents. In fact, it was not long before workers began to correspond with the Countess directly and even her oldest son Francis when he was of age could entrust his own property management to his mother.[10]

While wealthy, the Countess was nonetheless financially cautious, learning from the money troubles that had beleaguered her own family. Her correspondence with Lord Huntingdon included advising him on cutting back on unnecessary expenses and her resolution to do the same.[11] Selina's administrative abilities and attentiveness to money matters would prove useful in her

---

[10] Welch, *Spiritual Pilgrim*, 4.
[11] Welch, *Spiritual Pilgrim*, 23.

subsequent evangelistic ventures. We can witness God already preparing her for the work that lay ahead: be it securing funds for chapel construction, tirelessly sending out requests to ministers to support the pulpit ministry, or ensuring the smallest provisions were on hand for the students at her college—smoothly overseeing these duties was certainly no small feat and the Countess seemed to have effortlessly slipped into her succeeding role.

Family Life
Selina's letters to Lord Huntingdon also reveal her devotion to the children. Her prolonged illness meant that she was absent from them for months at a time. Writing from Bath, she expressed the torture of imagining the family together without her; her children being so young, she feared that their memory of her would begin to fade.

> 16 February 1731:
> My tenderest blessings are ever with those dear little babies I have left behind me, and it is an unspeakable delight to me to think the waters are likely to enable me to return to my dearest of Creatures, who is the very joy of my heart and pleasure of my eyes.[12]

> 13 March 1732:
> Oh could my dear imagine how I envy every creature that is near you and think them only happy. My dear little ones will I fear quite have forgot me but I must submit with reflecting that in the numbers of blessings I have, I must not think to live without a trial and though I am apt to think this a heavy one ...[13]

---

[12] Tyson, *Lady Huntingdon and Her Correspondence*, 24.
[13] Tyson, *Lady Huntingdon and Her Correspondence*, 27.

Portrait of the Wife and Mother

30 March 1732:
I beg my dear Life will let me know if my dearest Frank ever talks of me and whether you think he will remember me for I dread losing that share in his warm heart I once had ... My tenderest blessings are with my little ones and a thousand kisses to them and imagine a million to yourself.[14]

In spite of the distance between them, Selina did what she could to bring the children comfort and pleasure, generously sending them toys and inquiring to Theophilus regarding their needs. On one occasion, her arrangement to send a parcel of goodies to the children had failed because it was too heavy to be transported.[15]

By 1740 her eldest sons Francis, George, and Ferdinando were all away at the Westminster School in London. Mother and sons maintained correspondence, sometimes at the Countess' urging since she so eagerly wanted to be involved in their lives. In fact her consistency in letter-writing once prompted her eldest son to chide her when she had briefly neglected the habit.[16] While the boys were away, Selina remained the attentive mother, following closely her sons' progress in school, recommending books, offering rewards for studiousness, sending them allowances for treats and clothing, and advising them to dress appropriately for the weather so they would not catch a cold.[17]

The Countess' daughters Elizabeth and Selina and the youngest Henry stayed with their mother. A tutor was hired to instruct them at home, so all the Hastings children were sufficiently educated.[18] The eldest daughter was proving to be bright and

---

[14] Tyson, *Lady Huntingdon and Her Correspondence*, 28.
[15] Tyson, *Lady Huntingdon and Her Correspondence*, 26, Letter to Theophilus, March 8, 1732.
[16] Methodist Archives Centre, Drew University, Madison, New Jersey, Hunt. A 94, Lady Huntingdon to Frank, 24 [? 1739], quoted in Welch, *Spiritual Pilgrim*, 28.
[17] Methodist Archives Centre, Drew University, Madison, NJ, Hunt. A 84, Lady Huntingdon to son, 19 March 1745, quoted in Welch, *Spiritual Pilgrim*, 28.
[18] Cook, *Countess of Huntingdon*, 50.

knowledgeable, and in the Countess' letters to Francis, the youngest daughter was depicted as a ball of amusement: "Your little sister is most extremely ridiculous and entertaining" [dated 4 October 1740] and "Your Papa sends all of you his and your sister Elizabeth her love. Your little one is most extremely ridiculous and will make you laugh very much when you see her."[19]

There is no doubt that Lady Huntingdon was most happy when the whole family was together, and a sampling of her letters demonstrates the closeness between them even when they were apart. The siblings themselves possessed similar fondness for one another. The Countess' letter below pictures little Selina making a homemade gift for her brother while he was away at school:

> 1 September 1740/41:
> Little Selina asks if brother Hastings is coming and that she loves him dearly and dear brother Ferdy and bids me tell you she is sewing a piece of rag, these are her own words... As soon as I dare let her, your sister [Elizabeth] shall write to you till which time she is affectionately yours. I am truly thankful my dear Ferdy is so well over his cough and desire my blessing to him. I am my dear, dear, dear, Jewel most tenderly yours.[20]

The approaching holidays was a time of anticipation for the Hastings family as brothers and sisters would soon be united, as the Countess reminds Francis in a letter written in the fall of 1740:

> You are, my dear child, very good in letting me hear from you so often and I fail not to praise God for your being so well. I hope a short time will enable me to see you, our intent being to see Enfield now very soon and stay till your holidays are over that those may be spent with us there. I am very sure this will give you great pleasure. I think to bring

---

[19] Tyson, *Lady Huntingdon and Her Correspondence*, 36.
[20] Tyson, *Lady Huntingdon and Her Correspondence*, 37.

Portrait of the Wife and Mother

up with me your sisters and your little brother that we may be all together.[21]

It appears that Lord Huntingdon was not excluded from these familial affections. In 1740 when the children were suffering from coughs, the Countess was confident that their spirits would immediately be lifted upon seeing their father:

> The children are as well as can be expected but their coughs are bad. I hope I shall be able to give you some better accounts of us all, and that we shall soon have the joy of seeing you, which will do more to making us all better than anything else can do.[22]

While concluding a letter to Theophilus, Selina confessed that if the children were privy to her business they would have certainly pestered her, anxious to dictate their own messages to their father: "The Children, did they know all I was writing, would be full of their commissions for me but fancy some intend writing."[23]

Admittedly Selina's bonds with all her children were not always as warmly depicted as these early years, this especially evident in her relationships with her eldest son Francis and daughter Elizabeth. As conscientious as Selina may have been in tending to the needs of her children, her strong and assertive character may have been at times too much for some of them to bear. The narrative surrounding her conversion we will soon learn, but this pivotal event that took place in 1739 which had drastically transformed her life and the direction it was to take had its own impact on the family.

Elizabeth, for instance, complained that her mother was becoming "righteous overmuch," a description that was used to

---

[21] Tyson, *Lady Huntingdon and Her Correspondence*, 36.
[22] Tyson, *Lady Huntingdon and Her Correspondence*, 35.
[23] Tyson, *Lady Huntingdon and Her Correspondence*, 40, October 4, 1746.

identify early converts in the Methodist movement. Aligning with public sentiment, Elizabeth held a critical view of her mother's religion. The blossoming adolescent who was demonstrating to be a vibrant and gregarious character, was feeling more and more the constraints of being at home; deeply drawn to the revels of court life, she much preferred to be in the company of her contemporaries. This ran contrary to the more serious and responsible lifestyle Selina preferred for her daughter. Exasperated from being under her mother's rule, Elizabeth broke away as soon as the opportunity arose: in 1752, at twenty-one-years-old, she married Lord Rawdon and moved to Ireland. The Earl was significantly older than Elizabeth, but Selina considered it a consolation that her son-in-law was a "sensible and worthy" man.[24] The marriage appears to have been a happy one as Elizabeth affirmed in a letter written to Francis not long after the marriage.[25]

Francis himself had also matured into a bright, talented, charming young man, attuned to the social graces of high society. As the expectant heir of the reputable Hastings family, this, of course, did not go unnoticed. Many in his circle began to express their esteemed impressions of him, in particular, a Lord Chesterfield, who relished in the prospect of molding Francis into a worthy and refined gentleman (which for Lord Chesterfield was not without its own benefits).

Although the specter of the aristocratic stage never seemed to have a firm hold on the Countess, she could not resist the adulation Lord Chesterfield heaped on her son. The influential nobleman was not only clever and alarmingly skillful in winning the approval of his fellow aristocrats but was also known for his immoral living and antipathy towards religion. Perhaps lured by his eloquence and well-mannered disposition, the Countess made the

---

[24] Rylands MS., Letter 21, quoted in Cook, *Countess of Huntingdon*, 167.
[25] Cook, *Countess of Huntingdon*, 167.

Portrait of the Wife and Mother

regretful mistake of allowing such a man to be an adviser to her son.[26] By the age of 20, Francis was already indulging in the privileges of his position and it was no secret that he did so irresponsibly. Travelling abroad, he had formed illicit liaisons with women, and on top of bringing shame to his mother, he seldom kept in contact with her. But the only admonition Lord Chesterfield gave to Francis regarding his conduct was that he ought to avoid committing offenses that would cause him to fall out of favor with those who held the power to affect his standing—his mother included.[27]

A Mother's Prayer

The deepest expression of Selina's love for her children was her hope and prayers for their salvation. Letters written to Francis when he was away at school attest that this was her wholehearted plea. A few years after her conversion, Selina wrote the following to her teenaged son:

> 1 March 1742:
> My greatest delight on this side of heaven would be the warm desires your heart might have to love and serve God that you may wear a never fading crown of glory. Think of this my dear, dear, Jewel and then how poor will all things seem to you when you look further in the heavens eternal and unchangeable that is reserved for you, and this if you do not reject it, purchased by the Son of God for you.[28]

When the occasion arose, ministers who labored alongside her during the Revival reached out to them. John Wesley, who became a spiritual adviser and friend to the Countess following her

---

[26] Cook, *Countess of Huntingdon*, 167–169.
[27] Tyson, *Lady Huntingdon and Her Correspondence*, 41, Letter from Lord Chesterfield to Francis, Lord Huntingdon, September 29, 1750.
[28] Tyson, *Lady Huntingdon and Her Correspondence*, 38.

conversion, had early on preached to Francis and Elizabeth.[29] In the years to come, Francis, intelligent and self-assured, presuming that he understood enough of the Christian religion to enter into a debate about it, engaged in such discussion with his mother's trusted friends. William Grimshaw (1708-1763) in 1755 concluded one such exchange by cutting to the heart of the problem: "... argument will do you no good. If you really needed information I would gladly assist you. But the fault is not in your head but in your heart, which can only be reached by divine power."[30]

Next to the "one object of [her] heart"—her blessed Saviour—the wellbeing of her family and the state of their souls were what most concerned her. Her children George, Selina, and Henry would eventually show evidence of true saving faith.[31] Francis, though maintaining a distance from his mother's work during the Revival, nonetheless expressed his acceptance of his mother's spiritual calling on at least two occasions. When the Countess was building her chapels in the 1760s, a bishop wrote to Francis protesting against it, beseeching that the son do something to suppress his mother's work. Francis replied: "Gladly ... but will you do me the favour to inform me what to urge, for my mother really believes the Bible."[32] When the Countess in the 1780s saw mounting opposition to the operation of her chapels, Francis wrote a letter of concern to his mother, and Selina's response demonstrates that even amidst trial her great concern was to be a godly testimony to her son:

> ... your kind concern loses not the gratitude so much its due from me on this occasion. Fear not, care not about me, my dear son; I have a faithful friend who has said "I will never leave nor forsake you, No that I never, never will." I have

---

[29] Cook, *Countess of Huntingdon*, 113.
[30] Cook, *Countess of Huntingdon*, 192-193.
[31] Cook, *Countess of Huntingdon*, 87 (George), 214-216 (Selina), and 179 (Henry).
[32] Haweis, *Church History*, 3:254, quoted in Cook, *Countess of Huntingdon*, 344.

Portrait of the Wife and Mother

tried His promise often, and He has never failed me yet ... and because not more happily in my power to give greater proof of the warmth of my affection for you, you must believe I extremely love you.[33]

Elizabeth, too, was witness to her mother's spiritual character. In the 1770s, when a missionary project in America began to look pessimistic, Selina, too old to travel the distance across the Atlantic yet desiring to offer encouragement to the workers, arranged for a full-sized painting of herself to be sent there in hopes to enliven their spirits.[34] The portrait was a symbolic representation: the Countess stands in front of a small dark cave, a deliberate contrast to the tall stature of Selina whose gaze is serious and assured. Atop the cave is a plant that has just begun to flower and just beyond it a mighty tree. Her dress pointedly modest and coronet crushed underfoot cast aside all rank. Her right arm rests over the cave, hand grasping a laurel wreath that signifies victory. Elizabeth, the only child to outlive Selina, could concede that the artwork was an authentic depiction of her mother.[35] While she may not have shared in her mother's faith, her opinion of the portrait reveals she still recognized the spirit of her mother's life of Christian ministry.

---

[33] Tyson, *Lady Huntingdon and Her Correspondence*, 266.
[34] Cook, *Countess of Huntingdon*, 327.
[35] Cook, *Countess of Huntingdon*, 328.

4
Portrait of the Countess before Conversion

While Selina's conversion did not take place until her early thirties, snapshots of her childhood as recounted by Thomas Haweis testify that her spiritual hunger was long present. We can imagine a sensitive soul like Selina being overwhelmed by the boiling tensions in her family. How frequent and how open these conflicts were we can only speculate; but what is known is that Selina as a child often withdrew, taking refuge in a secluded place in her home. The young girl was anxious for relief, and in this quiet, solitary corner she poured out her worries to God.[1] For Selina, comfort was found in prayer.

Family hardship drove Selina to contemplate and seek after a world beyond her own. This longing for God was intensified by another childhood event. A nine-year-old Selina had been strolling one day and stumbled upon a funeral procession. Naturally curious, she looked on and beheld in the coffin a child about the same age as she. Selina could not keep away; she trailed behind it, observing the ceremony from a distance.[2] The scene left such a haunting impression on her that even after that day she continued to visit the child's grave. The body of a lifeless child became a mirror for what would inevitably become of her. Death had cast its fierce glare and invoked in Selina a view of the eternal. But once again—prayer was her source of solace: to God she would plead for deliverance from her earthly fears about her own mortality.

This hungering after the spiritual did not dissipate as the decades passed. Assuming her place in English society, the Countess could not help but feel the meaninglessness of its fleeting

---

[1] Cook, *Countess of Huntingdon*, 8.
[2] Cook, *Countess of Huntingdon*, 9.

The Bold Evangelist

pleasantries and amusements. During a stay in Bath for its curative waters, she did not hide her distaste for the lifestyle that presided there. She described the popular city as "the most stupid place I ever yet saw."[3] Bath had become a place of attraction for the indulgent rich. Many travelled there specifically for its social diversions, gambling being one favored pastime. Mingling with others of the nobility whose daily exchanges consisted of superficial banter wearied the Countess who not only yearned for the companionship of her husband and children but also for matters of greater spiritual substance.

Extravagant outfits, impressive estates, treasured art and book collections, the company of nobility, a reputation that brought with it coveted influence and respect—none of these ever fully satisfied the Countess. Time and time again she expressed her utter discontentment with the opulent lifestyle her position afforded. One of her letters written to Lord Huntingdon's half-sister Lady Betty on 27 December 1738, the year before her conversion, uncovers the Countess' estimation of the life she led: "... consideration must [show] us the emptiness of all [worldly] things without using this life as the way and means to lead us to a better... [I have] lived a life so disagreeable to [myself]."[4]

It is not surprising then that the Countess' generosity occurred even prior to her conversion. Granted, acts of charity were not uncommon among women of the aristocracy: in the act of giving these women gained greater control over the lower class, approval from their peers, and admiration that extended beyond their roles as wives and mothers. There were, however, women who were earnest in their giving, and the Countess was certainly one of them. She was heavily involved in philanthropic efforts more than a decade before her conversion. Seeing what was

---

[3] Tyson, *Lady Huntingdon and Her Correspondence*, 24.
[4] Cook, *Countess of Huntingdon*, 30.

Portrait before Conversion

stirring in her heart in the earlier part of her life helps to explain the zeal behind her actions. She was profoundly aware of the vain use of her time and resources and longed to use these for a greater purpose. What dramatically changed following her conversion was that her contributions shifted significantly toward the Methodist cause.

In the area of philanthropy the Countess' role model was her sister-in-law Lady Betty who was twenty-five years older than Selina.[5] Both women were loyal members of the Church of England, though at this stage neither of the women were converted.[6] Lady Betty donated each year to the Church of England and its affiliated outreach organizations, the Society for the Propagation of the Gospel (SPG) and the Society for Promoting Christian Knowledge (SPCK). Lady Betty's deep regard for education moved her to support the establishment of schools as well as those who aspired to become ministers but who could not afford to attend the universities. Worth noting is that one well-known student who studied at Oxford University whom Lady Betty supported was George Whitefield.[7]

Selina must have appreciated having a figure like Lady Betty in her life—someone who was not only family but also equally dedicated to religious and humanitarian ends. Like her sister-in-law, the Countess donated to organizations like SPCK, and as early as 1728 she was purchasing Bibles and other religious literature to give out to those in and around her Donington Park home. When Lady Betty asked for her financial support for a needy cause, she assented.[8] The Countess also showed compassion for the poor and sick. She was one of the donators to the newly established Foundling Hospital in the late 1730s, a home that cared and

---

[5] Welch, *Spiritual Pilgrim*, 33.
[6] Cook, *Countess of Huntingdon*, 18.
[7] Welch, *Spiritual Pilgrim*, 34.
[8] Welch, *Spiritual Pilgrim*, 35.

provided future education for infants neglected or left abandoned on the streets of London.⁹ Schools were also set up by the Countess to offer instruction for impoverished families.

Even at this point, Selina remained a stranger to the gospel. She still believed that God's favor was earned by her good works. Yet deep within her must have been awareness that this was vastly inadequate, as she professed in one letter, "I would undergo everything to come to the true knowledge of my Saviour."¹⁰ This cry of Selina's heart before her conversion is much like many of those who would become leaders in the Evangelical Revival, namely George Whitefield, John Wesley, Charles Wesley, and Benjamin Ingham. In order to arrive to the narrative of the Countess' conversion, it is to these men's stories we must first turn.

---

[9] Cook, *Countess of Huntingdon*, 30.
[10] Cook, *Countess of Huntingdon*, 34.

5
The Conversion of the Countess and Some Methodist Leaders

To better understand the circumstances of Selina Hastings' conversion, the focus must shift momentarily to a group of spiritually hungry men at the University of Oxford.

In the fall of 1729 at Oxford University, a man named Charles Wesley (1707-1788) formed a group that became known as the Holy Club. As its title implies, the group's aim was to encourage its members to live more religiously upright lives. John Wesley (1703-1791), Charles' older brother, eventually assumed leadership of the Holy Club. While the brothers were equally devoted to the club's spiritual pursuits, John, already a tutor at the university and a Fellow of Lincoln College, was the born leader. Charles was endowed with other qualities: his warm, easygoing, and sensitive nature attracted many friends.

Two prominent recruits of the Holy Club were George Whitefield (1714-1770) and Benjamin Ingham (1712-1772). Upon entry into Oxford in 1732, George's situation was not as fortunate as that of the Wesley brothers who were the sons of an Anglican minister at the Epworth Rectory in Lincolnshire. George's family ran an inn in Gloucester, but following the death of his father when he was a young child, business at the inn deteriorated. Unable to afford tuition at Oxford, he was admitted by working as a servitor performing odd jobs for a handful of the more affluent students. His position at the university segregated him from the others; but a year later, when it was discovered that he possessed similar aspirations as the men of the Holy Club, Charles invited George to join them. George held its members in high esteem:

Never did persons strive more earnestly to enter in at the strait gate. They kept their bodies under, even to an extreme. They were dead to the world, and willing to be accounted as the dung and offscouring of all things, so that they might win Christ. Their hearts glowed with the love of God and they never prospered so much in the inner man as when they had all manner of evil spoken against them. ... I now began, like them, to live by rule, and to pick up the very fragments of my time, that not a moment of it might be lost.[1]

All members of the Church of England, these men endeavored to support one another as they made every effort to live dutifully religious lives. Besides holding regular Bible studies and prayer meetings, the group fasted twice a week, received Holy Communion every week, helped the poor, visited the sick and imprisoned, and poured themselves into painstaking self-examination with the intent of making the best use of their time. The zealous behavior of these men was so peculiar to the other students at the university that it provoked ridicule. Their peers branded them such derogatory labels as "Bible Moths," "Bible Bigots," "Enthusiasts," and "Methodists." It was this final one that would later identify the Methodist movement. The label alluded to the group's strict and *methodical* observance of their Anglican beliefs and practices.

Scrupulous in their actions, these men—sincere and well-intentioned—believed that their good works earned the favor of God. They thought that the more firmly they stuck to this regiment of strict spiritual discipline, the closer they came to the salvation of their souls. But at the end of it, each of them would confess that he experienced no true joy or peace. As the narratives of their conversions uncover, no matter how hard they tried to secure salvation on their own terms, they were left feeling apprehensive and dejected by the futility of their efforts.

---

[1] Arnold A. Dallimore, *George Whitefield: God's Anointed Servant in the Great Revival of the Eighteenth Century* (Illinois: Crossway, 1990), 16.

Conversion of the Countess

George Whitefield's Conversion

In the fall of 1734, prior to his conversion, George Whitefield had subjected himself to extremes in the pursuit of self-denial. He went around the Oxford campus in a disheveled state and his excessive fasting left him emaciated. He uttered few words and spent weeks lying prostrate on the ground in prayer. His academics began to suffer. So weak was his body that he could barely move about on his own. Those on campus thought he had lost his mind. By the spring of 1735, the deterioration of his condition resulted in the doctor confining him to bed for seven weeks. Even then he forced himself to keep a record of his sins and confessed them to God day and night.

Yet it was not until his situation became hopelessly bleak that Whitefield was delivered. He came to understand that nothing he did, no matter how radical or remarkable, could contribute to the salvation of his soul. Before his conversion he had sought to adhere to the teachings of William Law, whose book *A Serious Call to a Devout and Holy Life* focused on man's pious works as the way to acceptance with God. It was another book, however, that started him on the path towards conversion, Henry Scougal's *The Life of God in the Soul of Man*, which taught that "true religion was union of the soul with God, a real participation of the divine nature, the very image of God drawn upon the soul." The love of God, finding its deepest expression in the sacrifice of his Son on the Cross for sinful men, "makes the soul resign and sacrifice itself wholly unto him, desiring above all things to please him, and delighting in nothing so much as in fellowship and communion with him, and being ready to do or suffer any thing for his sake, or at his pleasure." Good works, charity toward humankind, and godly obedience sprung from a personal response to this divine love; they were not to be reduced to tireless, vain human effort.

It was shortly after Easter in 1735 that George realized he could do nothing to save himself and at last put his faith and trust in the grace of the gospel: "God was pleased to remove the heavy load, to enable me to lay hold of his dear Son by a living faith, and by giving me the Spirit of adoption to seal me even to the day of everlasting redemption."[2]

The Conversion of the Wesley Brothers

The conversions of John Wesley, Charles Wesley, and Benjamin Ingham took place following their boarding a ship to Georgia in the fall of 1735. At the invitation of its governor James Oglethorpe, the trip was a missionary endeavor to reach the Indian people in the newly established American colony. The men's desire stemmed not only from a spiritual concern for the colony's people but also the state of their own souls. For them the hardships that came along with the mission tended to the latter. The voyage turned out to be a failure. John, after his conversion, would later say of the mission: "I left my native country in order to teach the Georgian Indians the nature of Christianity. But what have I learned myself in the meantime? Why ... that I who went to America to convert others was never myself converted to God."

But it was because of this voyage that each of these men came to the realization Whitefield had a few years earlier: salvation was not achieved by outward action but by inner transformation. This realization came from witnessing the godly conduct of the Moravians who were travelling with them. At one point the ship encountered a series of vicious storms that wrought fear in almost everyone onboard—all except the Moravians. This group of Germans, comprising both adults and children, were instead calmly singing a hymn. The men were moved by the stark contrast between their internal turmoil and the unwavering assurance of the Moravians. Asked to give an explanation for their assurance, the Moravians' answer was Christ. Christ was their assurance.

---

[2] Dallimore, *George Whitefield*, 18.

Conversion of the Countess

It was later Peter Böhler (1712-1775), a German Moravian missionary, who explained to the Wesley brothers the need for a "new birth." The brothers, wearied and disillusioned by their mission, were being told by Böhler that believing in Christianity was far from being a burden. He taught them that salvation was by grace alone: it takes place the moment an individual, recognizing that he is a sinner and needs to be reconciled with God, puts his faith in Christ; Christ's atoning work on the Cross grants the sinner complete forgiveness.

For Charles Wesley the transformation took place on 21 May 1738. He wrote in his journal, "I now found myself at peace with God, and rejoiced in hope of loving Christ." Humbled by this awakening, Charles, who would come to write as many as 7,000 hymns in his lifetime, expressed his sheer wonder in the first verse of one of his most famous hymns, "And Can it Be that I Should Gain":

> Died He for me, who caused His pain?
> For me, who Him to death pursued?
> Amazing love! How can it be
> That thou, my God, shouldst die for me?

For John the turning point took place several days later at a Moravian meeting place in London known as the Fetter Lane Society. After hearing a message, he noted down his marked response: "I felt my heart strangely warmed. I felt that I did trust in Christ, Christ alone, for salvation; and an assurance was given me that he had taken away my sins, even mine, and saved me from the law of sin and death."

Benjamin Ingham's Conversion

Like the Wesleys, Benjamin Ingham was deeply affected by the Moravian missionaries. After his return to England from the

The Bold Evangelist

Georgian mission, he met with Whitefield in England and learned of his ministry while he and the others were away in America.[3] The conversations between the two men on their spiritual awakenings and the sharing of their excitement about proclaiming the gospel of free grace must have been as encouraging as it was invigorating. The effect of Whitefield's preaching was reverberating throughout England—in Bristol, Bath, London, and Gloucester— vast numbers were flocking to hear the young preacher.

After much prayer, Ingham felt called to go back to his homeland in Yorkshire. Like Whitefield, he preached with vigor and endurance the message of the new birth, unheard of by the Yorkshire residents. Very soon the message spread and caught the attention of the Countess of Huntingdon's sisters-in-law; the curiosity of Ladies Margaret, Anne, and Frances were piqued and soon Ingham was invited to preach at the Hastings sisters' private chapel at Ledston Hall.[4] Imagine the sisters listening attentively to Ingham describing his earlier life steeped in formal religion and then his encountering the godly testimony of the Moravian Christians on the boat to Georgia.[5] Ingham's ministry to the Hastings sisters was about to cause a ripple effect in the Evangelical world.

The Conversion of Selina Hastings

Weeks later at Donington Park the Countess received a letter from Lady Margaret with the incredible news: she, along with Ladies Anne and Frances, had now found assurance in Jesus Christ, her "Dear Redeemer." Around the early summer of 1739 the Earl and Countess made a brief visit to Ledston Hall in Yorkshire; there Selina witnessed firsthand the change in Lady Margaret who eagerly shared with her: "Since I have known and believed in the

---

[3] Cook, *Countess of Huntingdon*, 28.
[4] Cook, *Countess of Huntingdon*, 28–29.
[5] Cook, *Countess of Huntingdon*, 34.

Conversion of the Countess

Lord Jesus Christ for salvation, I have been as happy as an angel."[6] In Margaret then was a spiritual joy that Selina herself had not yet discovered but had always deeply longed for.

Although there is no record revealing the details surrounding the Countess' conversion, references to it emerge in a letter from Lady Margaret in 1739 as well as one to Charles Wesley in 1766, putting the date of Selina's conversion at the end of July 1739.[7] At the time Selina was coming out of another bout of illness and was pregnant with Henry. Pressing upon her still were the financial conflicts within her own family over her deceased father's estate, the pressures of managing her many properties, the challenges of raising six children under the age of ten (made difficult by the fact that she was frequently separated from them), and above all, the persisting dissatisfaction with her quest for religious fulfillment. It must have taken time for Selina to embrace the message of salvation by grace alone: she had spent most of her life abiding by the belief that it was her own righteous living that pleased God. Yet the restlessness she felt in her heart was undeniable. So was the newfound joy that she beheld in Margaret.

Soon it was the Countess' turn to send a letter to Ledston Hall. Lady Margaret was elated by its contents:

> [The letter] came to me just as I was sitting down to supper and though it was at that time, my heart was so raised with gratitude to the ever Blessed Jesus for the good work He had wrought in you that it was a pain to me not to repeat the first verse of Psalm 103, "Praise the Lord, O my soul."[8]

The ever striving Selina had at last become convicted of her need of a Saviour. Thomas Haweis recounted the event:

---

[6] Cook, *Countess of Huntingdon*, 36.
[7] Cook, *Countess of Huntingdon*, 36–37.
[8] Tyson, *Lady Huntingdon and Her Correspondence*, 29.

She felt an earnest desire, renouncing every other hope, to cast herself wholly upon Christ for life and salvation. She instantly from her bed lifted up her heart to Jesus the Saviour with this importunate prayer; and immediately all her distress and fears were removed.[9]

About a month later another letter from Lady Margaret alluded to the spiritual interest of Lord Huntington as she expressed her prayer for the power of God to work upon the souls of both her sister-in-law and her "dearest brother, who is as dear to me as my own soul."[10] In the Countess' own words in a letter to Lady Betty in the fall of 1739: "My heart daily rejoices and praises God that the Scriptures are become his whole study and I do think he has truly a humble heart and I am fully persuaded he does not think himself possessed of the least degree of merit."[11] The Earl's loving devotion to his wife might have stimulated a genuine inquisitiveness into the source of her newfound faith. Certainly he was understanding enough to consent to accommodating in their home the many religious figures belonging to the early part of the Revival, even when, as we shall learn, aristocratic peers were looking on with suspicion and disdain. While the ultimate spiritual state of Lord Huntingdon remains unknown, one of the Countess' letters to him the year after her conversion articulates her hopes of their one day reuniting upon death:

So absolutely are you the object of all my earthly pleasure, and I can even with delight carry you farther with me and flatter myself (though so unworthy as I am) that I shall be a witness of a great share of Glory whenever we must cross by death to be united here in the constant praise of that all wise and gracious God, that has so uncommonly blest us here on

---

[9] Aaron C.H. Seymour, *The Life and Times of Selina Countess of Huntingdon* (London: 1840), vol. 1, 15.
[10] Tyson, *Lady Huntingdon and Her Correspondence*, 29.
[11] Tyson, *Lady Huntingdon and Her Correspondence*, 31.

Conversion of the Countess

earth together. For I have neither wish nor desire but to know His will and faithfully to perform it with my dear, dear Jewel here on earth.[12]

Humility, wonder, and gladness characterize the Countess during this period. Though her temper still surfaced at times, the change in her character following her conversion was noticed even by her maid, who could remark over a year later that the Countess had not been in a passion for more than twelve months.[13] To one of the leaders of the Moravians, James Hutton (1715-1795), a dear friend and fellow laborer of the Wesley brothers, wrote of his impression of Selina upon meeting with her and her husband in the fall of 1740: "The Countess ... I found more eager to hear the Gospel than any one I ever saw before ... I look daily for its striking deep root in her heart."[14]

Selina professed to Lady Betty the perspective she now had on her life: "I feel every day there is no delight and pleasure in this world equal to the conviction of pious souls. It raises the heart so much above all earthly things." Amidst the Hastings sisters' delight over their sister-in-law's transformation, most striking was Lady Margaret's response in light of the incredible events that were to come as a result of Lady Huntingdon's conversion:

> I was quite overpowered with joy and thankfulness to infinite wisdom and goodness for manifesting himself in so extraordinary a manner to my dear brother and sister .... What a reviving cordial it is to my spirits to read the account you give. The vigorous start you have made promises great things.[15]

---

[12] Tyson, *Lady Huntingdon and Her Correspondence*, 33.

[13] Tyson, *Lady Huntingdon and Her Correspondence*, 48.

[14] Tyson, *Lady Huntingdon and Her Correspondence*, 48, Letter from James Hutton to August Spangenberg, Bishop of the Reorganized Moravian Brethren and assistant to Count Zinzendorf, November 1740.

[15] Cook, *Countess of Huntingdon*, 37.

The Bold Evangelist

Little did Margaret know how profound her words were to be.

6
The Countess and the Early Methodist Revival

The early part of the eighteenth century saw the conversions of George Whitefield, brothers John and Charles Wesley, Benjamin Ingham, and the Countess of Huntingdon. The weary existence of relying on good works for salvation had come to an end. These individuals had, at last, discovered the joy and peace of a new life in Christ. The spiritual reality in England, however, was far from this. This was the time of the gin epidemic, the liquor cheap and available at almost every street corner in London. Drunkenness and its downward spiral in the lives of its victims was not the only problem. Choking the English climate were the economic despair of an alienated lower class; a disturbingly flawed legal system that more often promoted rather than suppressed lawlessness; and diseases like smallpox, typhus, and tuberculosis ravaging families. Amidst these dismal conditions emerged the revival. Armed with the liberating truth of the gospel, the early Methodists were eager to make it known.

Reaction of the Clergy to Methodist Preaching

In 1738 Whitefield had joined the Wesleys in their Georgian mission but returned to England four months later for two reasons: he aspired to build an orphanage in Georgia and wanted to secure support for it, and he was to be ordained a priest in the Church of England. Bishop Martin Benson ordained him in January 1739. When Whitefield began preaching the gospel of God's grace in churches, however, the Anglican clergy was less than pleased. Nestled comfortably in their ranks within the Established Church, such leaders considered him an irksome interference. But early

The Bold Evangelist

Methodists like Whitefield could no longer tolerate the failure of these leaders to provide for the spiritual needs of its members, who were fed an inadequate religion reduced to drab theological discourse and a burdensome morality. Faith in the redemptive power of the Cross and hope in the Holy Spirit's transforming work in the inner life of the individual were unheard of from the parish pulpit. Far from being models of godliness, these leaders indulged in their roles within the Church, which granted them positions of power and wealth but with little accountability. With Whitefield's bold proclamation of the need for a new birth, door after door of churches shut on him. The Anglican minister was left with no choice but to find another way to preach the gospel message.

Since early 1737 Whitefield's ministry had become so popular that when preaching both the church interior and exterior were packed with keen hearers. The church doors closed to him yet faced with such a crowd, the solution came to Whitefield to preach in the open air as his friend Howell Harris (1714–1773) had done in Wales. Harris was not an ordained minister but a soul set aflame by the gospel and desiring to share the message by whatever means he could.[1] For an Anglican minister, open-air preaching was a radical move, but Whitefield believed that pleasing Christ surpassed any need to please men. This man, then, from relatively modest beginnings, quickly earned his reputation as a remarkably gifted speaker. Even those not receptive to the gospel found his presence irresistible. One spectator was Scottish philosopher David Hume; an agnostic, he could still describe Whitefield as "the most ingenious preacher I ever heard; it is worth going twenty miles to hear him."[2] Whitefield preached the gospel with incredible urgency. Countless hearers were convicted by his

---

[1] Dallimore, *George Whitefield*, 44.
[2] Cook, *Countess of Huntingdon*, 121.

The Early Methodist Revival

words and brought to tears. His sermons presented simple gospel truths, infused with impersonations of Bible characters and gripping anecdotes, heightened by intense emotion. Often a crowd could witness the earnest preacher himself overcome by the very truths he spoke. The Lord had endowed him with a mighty voice: standing on a mound in an open field, tens of thousands could hear Whitefield preach.

One such crowd was the Kingswood coal miners who lived just outside of Bristol. Here were among the poorest, most uneducated, most brute of England. Unthinkable it was for a clergyman to venture to a place that likely meant his endangerment, even death. But venture is what Whitefield did. Clad in the gown of a churchman, knocking on doors, he boldly informed men, women, and children that a sermon was to be preached upon the nearby hilltop. There in the bitter cold of February 1739 emerged two hundred from their mines, perhaps out of pure wonderment of why a man of such rank would take an interest in their lot. To the destitute, disregarded, and desperate came the words of Jesus: "Blessed are the poor in spirit, for theirs is the kingdom of Heaven." Soon two hundred grew to thousands, their response vividly depicted by the preacher:

> Having no righteousness of their own to renounce, they were glad to hear of a Jesus who was a friend of publicans and sinners, and came not to call the righteous but sinners to repentance. The first discovery of their being affected was to see the white gutters made by their tears which plentifully fell down their black cheeks as they came out of their coal-pits.[3]

Less than two months passed that witnessed the dramatic transformation the Spirit had wrought in this once forlorn area—

---

[3] Dallimore, *George Whitefield*, 47.

the cussing, drunken air gradually replaced by hymn-singing and prayer. But speaking obligations beckoned Whitefield to Wales, London and America; he needed someone to continue the work that God had begun amidst the miners. To John Wesley he turned for help. Not long after reading Whitefield's pressing letter urging him to come to Bristol, he arrived, though initially hesitant about the idea of preaching in the open air: "I could scarcely reconcile myself at first to this strange way of preaching in the fields ... having been all my life (till very lately) so tenacious of every point relating to decency and order, that I should have thought the saving of souls almost a sin if it had not been done in a church."[4] But Wesley soon welcomed it as an opportunity to reach the masses that would otherwise not hear the gospel:

> God in Scripture commands me, according to my power, to instruct the ignorant, reform the wicked, confirm the virtuous. Man forbids me to do this in another's parish; that is, in effect, to do it at all, seeing I have now no parish of my own, nor probably ever shall. Whom then shall I hear, God or man? ... I look upon all the world as my parish.[5]

Bidding farewell was not easy, Whitefield wrote in April:

> Tongue cannot express what a sorrowful parting we had. My heart was so melted, that I prayed for them with strong crying and many tears. About one, I was obliged to force myself away ... What gives me the greater comfort is the consideration that my dear and honored friend, Mr. Wesley, is left behind to confirm those that are awakened, so that, when I return from Georgia, I hope to see many bold soldiers of Jesus Christ.[6]

---

[4] Nehemiah Curnock, *Journal of John Wesley*, vol. 2, March 31, 1739, 167, quoted in Turnbull, *Reviving the Heart*, 60-61.
[5] *The Journal of the Reverend John Wesley*, vol. 1, June 1739, 138.
[6] Jay P. Green, Sr., *George Whitefield's Journals*, 151.

The Early Methodist Revival

John Wesley laboured in the area for much of his life, raising up a school and assembling Methodist societies (groups of Christ followers that met weekly for Bible study, prayer, hymn-singing, and confession with the express desire to nurture one another's souls). It was Whitefield's open heart and oratorical power that lit the flame and John Wesley's leadership and organizational mastery that would sustain it. The two men started off as collaborators in the early Methodist Revival, but that bond was soon to be tested, as we shall later find out, when their theological differences came to the fore.

Reaction of the Nobility to the Countess' Conversion

As the aristocratic community learned of the influence of Methodist preaching on the Countess of Huntingdon and her conversion, expressions of disapproval quickly followed. The fervor with which Whitefield, the Wesleys, and Ingham preached was interpreted as fanaticism, even by Lady Betty, who was once unified with the Countess in her philanthropic and religious endeavors. Concerned about her sister-in-law's emotional and psychological state, Lady Betty sent her friend and adviser Rev. Thomas Barnard to counsel her. His letters in 1739 show his attempt to quell Selina's spiritual eagerness when he advised her to "observe moderation in all things," to "not pray too much," and to "not take on spiritual burdens and commitment."[7] The Countess' support of the Methodists had discredited her. For Lady Betty this was most pronounced when it was discovered following her death in December 1739 that Lady Huntingdon and the Earl were left almost entirely out of her will. Grieved Selina surely was, but the sunken expectations of receiving some of the Hastings estates caused her to scramble to manage the other estates, including the need to make provisions for her sisters-in-law Ladies Anne,

---

[7] Cook, *Countess of Huntingdon*, 38.

The Bold Evangelist

Frances, and Margaret who were then occupying Lady Betty's residence at Ledston Hall (their sister Lady Catherine had married in 1724 and died in 1740). Ledston Hall was to go to the Countess' eldest son Francis when he came of age but Lady Betty had left them no funds to maintain it, requiring the Countess to lease the estate.[8]

Ladies Anne and Frances relocated to Ashby Place near the Countess' Donington Park home, but Lady Margaret decided to stay behind in Yorkshire and it was then that her fondness for Ingham became obvious. Rumours had already been spreading about the pair, as one aristocrat wrote to another: "The news I have heard from London is that Lady Margaret Hastings has disposed of herself to a poor wandering Methodist."[9] Granted, displeasure with the union existed even within the family: Ingham was 12 years younger and the life of an itinerant preacher was not ideal for someone like Margaret.[10] When she and Ingham wed in November 1741, a temporary strain arose between her and Selina; but the spiritual bond between them was stronger and it was this bond to which Margaret appealed when reaching out to her sister-in-law: "I hope you will receive it as I write it, in love. For we have but one common Lord and Master, and all who are united in him will love one another."[11] Their friendship was soon rekindled.

Denunciation of the Methodists was shared by the Countess' younger sister Mary, Viscountess Kilmorey, who wrote to Selina a year after her conversion:

> I'm concerned to think that my dear sister who is so reasonable in everything else should encourage such a canting set of people who place their religion for the external show of it and pass uncharitable censures on them who are not in the

---

[8] Cook, *Countess of Huntingdon*, 46–47.
[9] Cook, *Countess of Huntingdon*, 48.
[10] Cook, *Countess of Huntingdon*, 47.
[11] Cook, *Countess of Huntingdon*, 67.

same way of thinking. But I hope God almighty, who once endued you with a very good understanding, will disperse the mist that now hangs over you and restore you to your former right way of judging.[12]

A letter from the Duchess of Buckingham reveals the challenge faced by the Countess when trying to share the gospel with those in her circle who thought that such religion was beneath them:

> I thank your Ladyship for the information concerning the Methodist preachers; their doctrines are most repulsive, and strongly tinctured with impertinence and disrespect towards their superiors in perpetually endeavouring to level all ranks, and do away with all distinctions. It is monstrous to be told that you have a heart as sinful as the common wretches that crawl on the earth. This is highly offensive and insulting; and I cannot but wonder that your Ladyship should relish any sentiments so much at variance with high rank and good breeding.[13]

Yet the Countess' sway remained apparent when, despite the Duchess' misgivings about the Methodists, she nonetheless accepted Lady Huntingdon's invitation to hear the Wesleys preach, expressing her intention even to bring along the Duchess of Queensbury.[14]

Selina's association with the Methodists had brought on shame to her family and disrepute among those of her rank. Yet her conviction was evident less than six months after her conversion when, at the insistence of his peers, Lord Huntingdon sent his friend and former tutor Bishop Martin Benson to address the conspicuous change in his wife. When the bishop tried to reason with her regarding the field preaching of Whitefield, the Wesleys,

---

[12] Tyson, *Lady Huntingdon and Her Correspondence*, 34.
[13] Cook, *Countess of Huntingdon*, 69.
[14] Cook, *Countess of Huntingdon*, 70.

The Bold Evangelist

and Ingham, she countered his accusations by reminding the bishop of his role and accountability to Jesus Christ and cited the Church of England's Articles and Homilies in her defense.[15] Short of words, Benson expressed how sorry he was to have ordained Whitefield, to which Lady Huntingdon replied: "My Lord, mark my words, when you come upon your dying bed, that will be one of the few ordinations you will reflect upon with complacence."[16] The spirit of this exchange was to reflect the character of the Countess' ministry for the rest of her life.

The Countess and Her Early Evangelistic Efforts

The early 1740s would see the beginnings of Lady and Lord Huntingdon's home at Donington Park becoming a setting for Methodist preaching to the nobility, though it was still some years before the Countess' appointment of her most notable chaplain George Whitefield. Her distinctive ministry still to take shape, Selina's hunger to reach unsaved souls was evident soon after her conversion, and while her highborn connections were attributed to drawing the ears of the rich in England, her concern most certainly was not restricted to those of her class. Local Methodist societies had received her financial support and so had the foreign missionary ventures and orphanage of the Moravians. Workers on her estate were urged to contemplate the state of their souls and to look to Christ for salvation and her servants were read religious literature. Her once dreaded trips to Bath for health reasons turned into occasions to share about her faith. The Countess' concern for the souls of the needy was seen when, heartened by the fruit that had taken place in Kingswood, she persuaded John Wesley to preach to the miners in Leicestershire near her home, which he did in May 1742.[17] When the growing effects of his ministry

---

[15] Cook, *Countess of Huntingdon*, 40.
[16] Cook, *Countess of Huntingdon*, 41.
[17] Cook, *Countess of Huntingdon*, 64–65, 76.

The Early Methodist Revival

there were criticized by the mayor, he credited Lady Huntingdon for the divine work that was stirring in northern England:

> When I was first pressed by the Countess of Huntingdon to go and preach to the colliers in and near Newcastle, that objection immediately occurred, 'Have they no churches and ministers already?' It was answered [by the Countess], "They have churches, but they never go to them! And ministers, but they seldom or never hear them! Perhaps they may hear you. And what if you save (under God) but one soul?" I yielded.[18]

This final question—What if you save but one soul?—surely remained at the forefront of her mind as she along with her Methodist allies began to face hostility for their evangelistic efforts. A letter from a mining contractor, for example, had warned her about a possible riot breaking out should she attempt ministry in the area.[19] A letter to her friend Philip Doddridge in the late 1740s confirms that mob violence was indeed a real threat: "Our affronts and persecutions here, for the Word's sake, are hardly to be described ... They called out in the open streets for me, saying, if they had me they would tear me to pieces." Yet she continued in the letter, "But this does but prove that it is the Lord that offends them, and so must he continue to the unregenerate heart."[20] Where she could exert her influence, the Countess appealed to civil magistrates about the persecution afflicting her Methodist friends, and in some instances was able to provide them protection. Selina's budding role in the initial part of the Revival was paving the way to a much larger one in the decades to come.

---

[18] John Wesley, *The Letters of the Rev. John Wesley* (London: Epworth, 1931), 2:14, quoted in Cook, *Countess of Huntingdon*, 81.

[19] Cook, *Countess of Huntingdon*, 64.

[20] *The Correspondence and Diary of Philip Doddridge* (London: 1830), vol. 4, 536, accessed November 2, 2015, eBook on Google Books.

7
Divisions and Bonds

While Selina Hastings had already put her trust in Jesus Christ and his redeeming work on the Cross to save her from her sins, a long journey still lay ahead: Selina was growing in her understanding of the Christian faith and how that worked out practically in her life. Personal doctrinal convictions had yet to be fully grasped and embraced. The Methodist movement arose with the shared belief in the life-changing power of the gospel, but within that movement were individuals that began to circulate considerably different views. The Countess was deeply enmeshed in the disagreements, having strong ties with many who were involved.

The Stillness Controversy
Brothers John and Charles Wesley were greatly indebted to the Moravians for their conversions. Together with Moravian leader Peter Böhler they had been meeting at the Fetter Lane Society in London since 1738. In fact, the society had become a spiritual home that drew George Whitefield, Howell Harris, Benjamin Ingham, and the Countess and Earl of Huntingdon. Anglican clergymen and lay leaders were worshipping alongside Moravians, united in their faith in Christ. For a time, these like-minded Christians enjoyed blessed, intimate fellowship.

But in the fall of 1739 when a Moravian by the name of Philip Henry Molther began propagating the doctrine of stillness, the Methodist movement witnessed its first break. Arriving to England, Molther was troubled by the intense religious expressions witnessed at the societies. He feared that there were individuals who were relying on these expressions to achieve salvation rather than relying on faith. He therefore emphasized "stillness," a doctrine that taught that an individual must remain "still" before God—that is, refrain from all means of grace, including reading Scripture, praying, fasting, doing good works, attending worship, and taking the Lord's Supper—until he or she possessed an absolute assurance of faith. No personal effort was to be counted on; the individual was to wait quietly for divine revelation. Any degree of uncertainty was unacceptable: either the individual was in the faith or not.[1]

John Wesley was appalled by the teaching, which contradicted his belief that there were indeed degrees of faith in the Christian life and the way to growing in the faith was by participating in the means of grace. The stillness doctrine was a threat to the spread of the gospel and the true teachings of Scripture and would inevitably lead to spiritual inactiveness and antinomianism (the belief that the gospel of free grace relieves the Christian from moral obligation). Not only was the teaching detrimental to the Methodist cause, but it also defied the very character of John who strongly upheld the importance of living an active Christian life in pursuit of holiness.[2]

In July 1740, John went his separate way and rallied his supporters. Months before, Ingham had come from Yorkshire to London in an attempt to prevent the split but to no avail.[3] The stillness doctrine was spreading, adopted by many, and Ingham came under Moravian influence and eventually put all his societies under Moravian leadership. The doctrine appeared to have enticed Charles Wesley as well, for Lady Huntingdon in a letter written to John Wesley in October 1741 revealed that it was she who steered his younger brother away from it:

---

[1] Cook, *Countess of Huntingdon*, 53.
[2] Cook, *Countess of Huntingdon*, 53.
[3] Cook, *Countess of Huntingdon*, 54.

Divisions and Bonds

Since you left us the Still Ones are not without their attacks. I fear much more for him [Charles Wesley] than myself ... He seemed under some difficulty about it at first, till he had free liberty given him to use my name as the instrument in God's hand that had delivered him from them.[4]

Meanwhile John had formed a new society—the Foundery—and it was to be a place of worship for Methodists for the next four decades. The Huntingdons attended services at the Foundery whenever they were in town and a warm friendship soon developed between the Wesley brothers and Selina.[5]

The Countess' Friendship with the Wesleys

The friendship between Lady Huntingdon and the Wesleys likely started in the fall of 1740 when she began corresponding with the brothers regularly; in the letters she could express her gratitude for their ministry to her. In October 1741 she wrote to John, "I am sure God will reward you ten thousand times for your labour of love to my soul."[6] In addition to letters, that same year John paid the Countess a number of visits at her home in Enfield Chase where he ministered to her over food and exposition of biblical texts. In her letters to John she sought advice on how to interpret specific passages of Scripture; asked for his judgment on decisions such as the appointment of certain individuals in carrying out evangelistic work; and encouraged him in his ministry, "Your friends all here think of you, speak of you and esteem you highly and that you may long shine here as pattern to all that believe and share everlastingly in the highest joys of the Blessed."[7]

John's esteem for Lady Huntingdon was evident at this point in their relationship. He trusted her enough to send her his

---

[4] Tyson, *Lady Huntingdon and Her Correspondence*, 48.
[5] Cook, *Countess of Huntingdon*, 54.
[6] Tyson, *Lady Huntingdon and Her Correspondence*, 49.
[7] Tyson, *Lady Huntingdon and Her Correspondence*, 50.

journals for evaluation, for in March 1742 she could write, "Surely my Friend has a mind to exercise his gift of humility in an extraordinary manner, when he could once ask my opinion upon his Journal. That it will both delight and comfort me, I have no doubts, and I think nothing is left for me but to speak my heart, knowing the love God hath for you."[8] His esteem was also demonstrated in the dedication of his second journal publication to her, aware that the title of the highly regarded Countess of Huntingdon on his work would attract a wider readership. The same could be said of his 1744 release *A Collection of Moral and Sacred Poems,* in which John revealed was inspired by Lady Huntingdon who, despising the content of contemporary poetry, had longed to see a set of English poems that focused the mind on the beautiful and pure.[9] Moved to invite people into her home and provide them biblical instruction, the Countess first solicited John's advice regarding her permitted role as a woman:

> I am going ... to take some of the most extreme poor that are simple of heart under my care and have them come twice a week. Pray the Lord that He may bless this. May I explain the Scriptures? Or how will you direct me? When they are fit I shall put them in bands. May I venture upon such an office? Speak plainly; I feel no will.[10]

Charles Wesley, however, was eventually the brother with whom Selina would form the deeper friendship. He was thoughtful and understanding, a poet at heart. John, fully immersed in evangelistic activity, left little time for the nurturing of his relationships and was often perceived as more rigid and aloof. To Charles, Selina could open up about her spiritual struggles. She

---

[8] Tyson, *Lady Huntingdon and Her Correspondence,* 51.
[9] Tyson, *Lady Huntingdon and Her Correspondence,* 71, Letter from John Wesley to the Countess, August 1744.
[10] Tyson, *Lady Huntingdon and Her Correspondence,* 53.

turned to him, for instance, when one of her close friends Fanny Cowper was dying; Fanny's godly faith and character, witnessed in her final hours, left a profound impression on Selina:

> It is easily seen [Fanny] loves to have me and me only do all things for her but never shows or expresses any anxiety if I do not. All her broken sleeps are only for fresh supplies of strength for prayer, singing or reading, and when she awakes out of them it is with a verse or line of a hymn... Should she continue long she will convince all who are not already convinced. Cease not to pray for us. This witness in death may add many souls to the faith.[11]

When Fanny died, Selina fought to come out from her despair, confessing to Charles in June 1742: "...no event could have happened that could have showed me my own heart more. I found so evil an impatience that my outward hope of my seeing her die in triumph was not answered that I was for a time only looking about me, and said, 'how can these things be?'"[12] The same letter presents a raw and tender depiction of Selina in her time of darkness:

> I feel no desire after anything in life ... I find neither freedom nor ease to go among the servants either to pray or read. I find myself alone. I live without either giving glory to God or good to man ... could anyone see the distress of my heart while my outward man seems to think of nothing, it would amaze anyone ... My heart has not lost the spirit of prayer but it is like praying to God afar off. I force myself into all means of grace but often am so dead that I meanly mock God. I trust I shall be refreshed by the coming of some of the faithful in the Lord.[13]

---

[11] Tyson, *Lady Huntingdon and Her Correspondence*, 56.
[12] Tyson, *Lady Huntingdon and Her Correspondence*, 57.
[13] Tyson, *Lady Huntingdon and Her Correspondence*, 59.

Charles too experienced periods of melancholy which he likewise confided to his dear friend, and so the two kindred spirits found encouragement from each other in their spiritual walks, Selina's letters to Charles numbering the most among all her surviving correspondence with friends.

This confidence developing between Selina and the Wesley brothers during the early 1740s meant that they played an influential role in her theological understanding of the Christian faith. On many occasions their guidance was invaluable, but one of their teachings posed a struggle for Selina—Christian perfection—and would eventually steer her toward forming closer bonds with Howell Harris and George Whitefield who rejected the doctrine.

Christian Perfection

John Wesley believed that through the Christian's journey of committing himself completely to God, it was possible to eventually become free of sin during this earthly life. This was accomplished through the sanctifying work of God by the Holy Spirit. As the individual practiced greater and greater discipline and obedience and as God poured his love into the believer's life, perfection in the Christian life could be achieved.

Selina held onto this teaching in the early years of her conversion, so much so that she could write to John in October 1741: "I have desired [Charles] to enclose to [the Moravians] your [sermon] on Christian Perfection. The doctrine therein contained I hope to live and die by. It is absolutely the most complete thing I know."[14] When Lady Huntingdon had converted in 1739, Whitefield had left for Georgia soon after. A chance encounter in Gloucester in 1742 following his return to England, however, led to a discussion on the doctrine, which Lady Huntingdon reported to John in February:

---

[14] Tyson, *Lady Huntingdon and Her Correspondence*, 48.

Divisions and Bonds

I told [Whitefield] I was so much happier than he was and that not from anything in myself but on my constant dependence upon Christ and next that I waited and hoped for an absolute deliverance from sin which he was willing to groan under always. He then said "pray does your Ladyship live without sin?" I told him "No!" but that there was such a state. He said none had ever yet done it, he was sure, that ever lived. But I made him own God was both able and willing and that before we died it was absolutely necessary we should be in it, and in this we only differ. I never could have received by anything that had been wrote against the doctrine, so strong a prejudice as his whole conversation was for it; although I must say he talked very sensibly; his manner agreeable, and command of words and smoothly put together.[15]

Selina—who had been wounded by a bitter past, who had ached for spiritual rest prior to conversion, who was the conscientious one—would have delighted in the possibility that she could one day be freed from sin. Yet as much as she desired to be persuaded by the doctrine, she had more trouble assimilating it. The reality of sin she faced day-in, day-out was oftentimes too much for her to bear. Deploring the sin in her life and longing to purge herself of it, she exclaimed to John in one letter, "I long to leap into the flames to get rid of my sinful flesh and that every atom of those ashes might be separate, that neither time, place, or person should say God's Spirit had ever been so clothed."[16] Peace and assurance eluded her while her depravity plunged her into despair: "I find myself weary of all things I do as it is all too little for God. Nothing satisfies me ... I am apt to be active at first in undertakings but when I find myself no nearer my end I proposed by it then I am

---

[15] Tyson, *Lady Huntingdon and Her Correspondence*, 50.
[16] Tyson, *Lady Huntingdon and Her Correspondence*, 49.

[timid]."[17] Selina would come to abandon the doctrine, for by 1747 Harris recorded in his diary, "[the Countess] was against sinless perfection, and the instantaneous gift of sanctification as the Bro. Wesleys hold."[18]

The shaky doctrine that the Wesleys persisted in teaching would see further conflict in the years to come. The problems inherent in subscribing to it inevitably emerged. In London, Methodists from Wesley's societies subsequently claimed that they had attained the aspired state of sinlessness. Exulting in their status, these individuals began to exercise their rule over those supposedly less perfect in their faith, declaring their powers to prophesize and to heal.[19] Many Methodist leaders opposing the unbiblical doctrine attributed the disorder to the Wesleys' teaching; in the ensuing decades John was obliged to clarify his meaning to appease his critics:[20]

> By perfection I mean the humble, gentle, patient love of God, and our neighbour, ruling our tempers, words, and actions. I do not include an impossibility of falling from it, either in part or in whole. ... And I do not contend for the term *sinless*, though I do not object against it.[21]

Beholding the effects of the teaching, Charles softened his position and treaded more cautiously while John remained fixed in his.[22] But there was a doctrine that stirred even greater controversy—predestination—represented in the dispute between the Wesleys and Whitefield.

---

[17] Boyd Stanley Schlenther, *Queen of the Methodists: The Countess of Huntingdon and the Eighteenth-Century Crisis of Faith and Society* (Durham: Durham Academic Press, 1997), 25.
[18] Cook, *Countess of Huntingdon*, 104.
[19] Cook, *Countess of Huntingdon*, 209.
[20] Cook, *Countess of Huntingdon*, 208.
[21] Cook, *Countess of Huntingdon*, 210.
[22] Cook, *Countess of Huntingdon*, 210.

Divisions and Bonds

Predestination

Recall Whitefield's preaching ministry in Bristol and how he had called on John to assume its leadership as he responded to needs elsewhere in the continent and America. Aware of their theological differences regarding the predestination and election doctrine, Whitefield prior to his departure had urged Wesley not to publicize it for fear of the damage it would do to their ministries. The two men remained unified in the gospel of grace and the transforming work of the Spirit in the believer's life; as Methodists they were dedicated to itinerant preaching and forming societies that would ensure the spiritual growth of converts. However, the divergence lay in their views on the role that God and the individual played in salvation.

Whitefield believed that from the beginning God had elected individuals for salvation, a position that is part of a theological system known as Calvinism (named after its proponent John Calvin, 1509-1564). God's choosing of the individual was not dependent on any human act but based on his unconditional love; the individual, then, having been divinely chosen, responds and can be assured that he or she will remain faithful until the end. Challenging this was the Arminian position (named after Jacob Arminius, 1560-1609)—advocated by John Wesley—which argues that the individual possesses complete freedom in choosing to trust Christ, for God from the beginning had chosen to save everyone (though only believers are redeemed). For the Arminian, an individual could reject God's call.

John did not heed Whitefield's advice. Shortly after his friend's departure in 1739 he published a sermon defending his Arminian position, fearing that the spread of Calvinism would not only undermine the need for preaching but result in loose Christian living—for if the individual was chosen by God, where was the motivation to preach, to pursue holiness? A refutation of these arguments was embodied in Whitefield himself, who preached confident that, while God elected, followers of Christ were the divinely appointed means of reaching the lost, and so they could be sure their evangelism would see results and that the lives of the converted would bear fruit. The two chief leaders of the Revival exchanged letters on the issue throughout 1740, yet Whitefield did not publish a response to John's sermon until a year and a half later. Whitefield's letter to John reveals why:

> If possible, I am ten thousand times more convinced of the doctrine of election, and the final perseverance of those that are truly in Christ, than when I saw you last. You think otherwise. Why then should we dispute, when there is no probability of convincing? Will it not, in the end, destroy brotherly love ...? How glad would the enemies of the Lord be to see us divided! ... how would the cause of our common Master every way suffer, by our raising disputes about particular points of doctrine![23]

Whitefield's impetus for publicly speaking out was because of the actions John had taken to blight the Calvinist position. Whitefield had returned to England only to find many from his former ministry challenging him. Early on Lady Huntingdon not only accepted the Wesleys' teaching on perfection but also on universal salvation. During that same chance meeting in Gloucester with Whitefield, she reported to John that the latter was also a point of discussion:

> [Whitefield] held forth above two hours, upon the doctrine of election and reprobation and collected all the choicest flowers of all that was to be gathered or said upon the several heads to charm me, telling withal (or giving me to understand) I was an elect. I told him upon what he said that upon

---

[23] Wood, A. Skevington, *The Inextinguishable Blaze: Spiritual Renewal and Advance in the Eighteenth Century* (Oregon: Wipf & Stock, 1960), 182.

Divisions and Bonds

the whole I found I should be such a looser by his way of thinking, that no consideration that I was yet able to see from anything he had said could have any weight. He seemed surprised and said "how could that be?" I told him I was so much happier than he was and that not from anything in myself but on my constant dependence upon Christ ...²⁴

A Widening Circle of Friends

Approaching the late 1740s Selina's position was to change as her company of friends began to include more Calvinists. Charles Wesley introduced Howell Harris to her in 1743. Initially intimidated by the Countess' status, he in less than a year could express to Whitefield his estimation of her prospective work in the Revival:

> Thursday night I had the favour of about four hours conversation with my Lady H. but where to begin to relate the mercies ... and benefits I had there, I can't tell. One so highly favoured and so fitted for the great work and place that I believe the Holy Spirit has called her.²⁵

At Harris' invitation, Lady Huntingdon began attending Moorfields Tabernacle, a wooden structure occupying the field where Whitefield first preached in London and built by friends who sought to provide a setting for Whitefield who was seeking refuge from John Wesley's campaign against his preaching on election. The two had attempted to reconcile in 1741, only to concede that their doctrinal differences made it unfeasible for them to work together. The Tabernacle was only a few miles from the Wesleys' Foundery, permitting Lady Huntingdon to partake in either of the

---

²⁴ Tyson, *Lady Huntingdon and Her Correspondence*, 50.
²⁵ Cook, *Countess of Huntingdon*, 93.

The Bold Evangelist

Methodist leaders' ministries.[26] Before long Whitefield shared with Harris his thoughts on the Countess who had become a regular at the Tabernacle:

> The good Countess has been there, and has been much pleased, I am told. She shines brighter and brighter every day ... My poor prayers will be daily offered up to the God of all grace to keep her steadfast in the faith and to make her a burning and a shining light.[27]

Around the same period Lady Huntingdon met Philip Doddridge (1702-1751). Known to us as the hymn-writer, Doddridge was a dissenting minister of a Northhampton church, and while his personal convictions led him to conduct his ministry outside of the Established Church, this did not keep him from worshipping and preaching together with Anglican clergymen like Whitefield at the Tabernacle.[28] The two ministers would in fact preach at each other's congregation, demonstrating that although differences could lead to division, it was possible to serve alongside one another and maintain bonds. And with Doddridge, Selina formed another. A letter to him in 1744 reveals her appreciation of her friends in Christ:

> We want not that friendship which the world has, discovering its degree by the mere outside shows of ceremony; but those hearts who know Him that was from the beginning, by this acquaintance can trace back the several other influences upon their minds ... and will not wonder such things should help them to maintain an esteem of mankind till a stronger motive supplies its place.[29]

---

[26] Cook, *Countess of Huntingdon*, 94.
[27] Luke Tyerman, *The Life of George Whitefield* (London: Hodder and Stoughton, 1877), 2:168, quoted in Cook, *Countess of Huntingdon*, 94.
[28] Cook, *Countess of Huntingdon*, 89-90.
[29] Tyson, *Lady Huntingdon and Her Correspondence*, 70-71.

Divisions and Bonds

The same letter uncovers a woman who was indeed growing in her faith and holding fast to the Word of God, as she judged the situation with the Moravians in light of the convicting power of divine truth:

> Here then, my friend, is what our Lord offers us. It is for such a religion I live, and in which, with his grace, I will die. This manifestation in the soul of Britain will prove as satisfactory as light is to the eye; and whenever this light appears equally great, there will be a perfect agreement; the degrees may and will cause disputes, as about the several imperfect objects a day dawn produces; and in this state the well meaning among the Moravians seem disputing with all who see differently with them. In this case our Lord's rule seems best, which was not to destroy error with evil, but by the establishment of truth, the rather to let it fall from its own weakness: exhort all sincere souls back, and the deadly thing will not hurt them though they drink of it.[30]

The early Revival bore witness to a number of divisions, most significant the split into the Calvinist Methodists and Arminian Methodists. Selina, crushed under the weight of perfection teaching, despairing over the realities of her sinful condition, began to take great comfort in the counsel and support of her growing community of friends.

---

[30] Tyson, *Lady Huntingdon and Her Correspondence*, 70–71.

8
Shattering Losses

Selina Hastings' work in the Revival was soon to take shape and a true servant was to emerge—devoted, passionate, and seemingly tireless as she labored more and more to bring the gospel to the unconverted. Yet Selina's faith and the hope and strength it granted her was not just seen in her public ministry but in her private life, a life that saw the passing of six of her children before her own, a life that left her a widow before she turned forty.

In the midst of trial, though shaken, Selina felt the assurance that rested on her newfound faith in her Lord and Saviour Jesus Christ. A year after her conversion, separated from her family once again and receiving news that her seven-month-old Henry, her youngest, was ill, she could declare her trust in the sovereign plan of her Heavenly Father:

> 28 July 1740:
> My dearest child may easily believe hearing of his not being well gave me great concern and it is with the greatest gratitude to Almighty God that you are so well recovered. Never having been from you in any illness before makes me lament now more than ever my distance from you. But I have such perfect confidence and faith in the Almighty's care over you that this is even made easy to me, that no evil or harm can happen to you without His permission and that willingly He will not afflict the children of men.[1]

This is not to make light of her suffering, for suffer she most certainly did. In April 1743, her third son Ferdinando died of smallpox at the age of eleven and her second son George died of the

---

[1] Tyson, *Lady Huntingdon and Her Correspondence*, 35.

The Bold Evangelist

same disease later that year just before turning fourteen. What was worse was that Selina was not there when Ferdinando's tragic death took place; he had been away at school and news about his illness had been withheld from the Countess for fear it would distress her already weak body. The horror she must have felt upon realizing that she had not been there to comfort her ailing child. In a letter to her husband she describes the heartache:

> Poor Ferdy has been the subject of my dreams many nights—this last particularly for no creature was ever so unhappy about another having to go through his whole sickness and death [alone]. It has made such an impression on me that in the midst of the most remote thoughts it jumps in and damps my spirits.[2]

Letters written before the death of her sons Ferdinando and George reveal the many promising hopes held in the heart of this young mother for her family. The Countess had expressed her joyful vision of watching the children grow up, becoming blessings to their father in old age.

> 29 April 1732:
> My tenderest blessings are with my dear children and as this day increases my wishes for my dear George and prayers for many happy and fortunate years and that when I am no more he may be a true and lasting blessing to his dearest Papa.[3]

> 2 January 1742:
> Your tenderness to those dear little Jewels will make the parting painful to you but it is great consolation to me that I believe no affection can be more warmly returned than I think was visible in those little souls to their dear Papa. I am persuaded that all of them that will be true and real blessings

---

[2] Cook, *Countess of Huntingdon*, 84.
[3] Tyson, *Lady Huntingdon and Her Correspondence*, 28.

Shattering Losses

to you will be continued to be the delight and pleasure of your old age.[4]

Sadly this would not be. Not even three years passed after the death of George and Selina would also lose her husband. In the year leading up to his death, Lord Huntingdon had begun to suffer from heart problems. He was set to journey to London to seek medical help but prior to his departure he had confided to his wife about a disturbing dream of his:

> He dreamed that death in the appearance of a skeleton, stood at the bed's foot; and after standing a while, untucked the bedclothes at the bottom, and crept up to the top of the bed (under the clothes) and lay between him and his lady.[5]

Before his death Selina had not been aware of the severity of her husband's condition. She could not bear the slightest possibility that he might have been unwell, yet she knew that her husband's protective love meant he was willing to suppress the truth to shelter her from pain. No, she could not risk it—so shortly after the Earl's departure she sent him a letter (the last one she would pen to him). Her impassioned plea attests that these were indeed two souls entwined:

> I hope you will, my dear creature, if you should find yourself the least ill, will allow it not to be concealed from me, for nothing could in this world make me so thoroughly unhappy ... Could my dear creature see the agonies of mind that at times I suffer on account both of your mortal and immortal part ... it would give you most sensible pain. My dear soul

---

[4] Tyson, *Lady Huntingdon and Her Correspondence*, 37.
[5] The Countess had revealed this to Augustus Toplady in 1776, which he recounted in his *Works* (London, 1794), 510, quoted in Cook, *Countess of Huntingdon*, 98. Toplady became acquainted with Selina in 1763 and was one of the ministers who preached at her chapels. Bond, *Augustus Toplady*, ch. 3.

will not think this is in the way of any reproof, but the fruit of my present tears that spring from the most ardent love.[6]

A week later, on 13 October 1746, Lord Huntingdon died of a stroke at the age of forty-nine. He was buried in St Helen's Church in Ashby-de-la-Zouch. The Countess was suddenly a widow with four children still to care for. Her husband of eighteen years, trusted lover and friend, was gone. She was to outlive the Earl by 45 years, but the agony of his loss remained with her—tears would fill her eyes at the mention of him.[7] This woman, whose strength and determination we will soon become more familiar with, was so affected by the circumstances she retreated from public life for months. Grief, Selina dealt with very privately; in her vulnerability she spoke little and shared little. But in such moments of weariness, we can appreciate brothers in Christ who offered her sacred counsel. The first one was from Howell Harris. Half a year after the Earl's passing, Selina seized the opportunity to speak with the Welshman during one of his visits to London. Their exchange reveals what was weighing on her heart at the time, which Harris recorded in his diary: "She consulted me about which was it best, to live retired and give up all, or fill her place, and I said the latter I thought was right whilst she felt she was able to be faithful and felt the Lord with her."[8]

The Countess, during similar times of trial, also received precious guidance from her friends John Berridge (1716–1793) and John Fletcher (1729–1785), ministers who supported her gospel ministry in the late 1750s. The contents of their letters offer us a glimpse inside the heart of a woman who was deeply hurting. Selina's youngest son Henry died in 1758 at the age of eighteen and her youngest daughter Selina in 1763 at the age of twenty-six. In

---

[6] Cook, *Countess of Huntingdon*, 98.
[7] Cook, *Countess of Huntingdon*, 99.
[8] Cook, *Countess of Huntingdon*, 103.

Shattering Losses

August 1758, feeling powerless in the decline of Henry's health (he had inexplicably lost his sight), she wrote assuredly to Charles Wesley, "All things work together for good and in this blind hope, under all the most unintelligible events, I rest secure, and am determined to make no explanations for myself or others."[9] Yet while she clung to the promises of God, a mother she still was. Her own daughter, while battling a violent fever, was worried about her mother's emotional state and tried to comfort her: "My dear mother, why not now; the Lord can make me ready for Himself in a moment and if I live longer I may not be better. I am a poor creature. I can do nothing myself. I only hope you will be supported."[10] When Lady Selina died, the Countess once again withdrew, utterly stricken by sorrow. William Romaine (1714–1795) at one point was obliged to reply to a letter on her behalf: "Although my Lady bears this so well, yet she feels it. She is but a woman, and though a gracious one, yet grace does not destroy nature. She is a parent and at present incapable of writing."[11] Feeling the weight of her absence from ministry, Berridge, a month later, felt it necessary to express these words:

> Is it not better to have your Selina taken to heaven, than to have your heart divided between Christ and Selina? ... She is gone to pay a most blessed visit, and will see you again by and by, never to part more ... but now she is gone to heaven 'tis almost intolerable. Wonderful strange love is this! Such behavior in others would not surprise me, but I could almost beat you for it, and I am sure Selina would beat you too, if she was called back but one moment from heaven, to gratify your fond desires. I cannot soothe you, and I must not flatter you. I am glad the dear creature is gone to heaven before

---

[9] Cook, *Countess of Huntingdon*, 179.
[10] Tyson, *Lady Huntingdon and Her Correspondence*, 103.
[11] Seymour, *Selina Countess of Huntingdon*, 1: 334, quoted in Cook, *Countess of Huntingdon*, 214.

you; lament if you please, but Glory, glory, glory, be to God.[12]

Forthright as he was, Berridge knew of the depth of Lady Huntingdon's faith and considered his friend's lingering misery uncalled for. Four months after her daughter's death, when Selina's state still had not improved, the compassionate words of Fletcher were needed to draw her out:

> Blessed be God for giving us the unspeakable satisfaction to see Lady Selina safely landed, and out of the reach of vanity. This is mercy rejoicing over judgment of a truth ... Come, my Lady, let us travel on, sticking close to our heavenly Guide; let us keep a hold of the hem of his garment by firmly believing the arms of his wise providence and everlasting love are underneath us; let us hasten to our friends in light ... Lord, Jesus, come quickly, and let us all be lost together in thy love and praise.[13]

Such are the bonds and activities of the faithful in the family of God. When one is seen to lose heart, another sees it as his godly duty to restore her confidence in the Lord Jesus. Tenderly these words are whispered to the weary soul, which by God's grace finds rest once again in the inexhaustible well of the Almighty Provider. The Countess was forced to move on without her beloved companion and the children who had been by her side, but many brothers and sisters in Christ ministered to her and encouraged her along the way. The loss of her dear ones most surely fortified her desire to use her life for the spiritual benefit of others, and Selina, now a widow, was free to pour herself into what she treasured most.

---

[12] Tyson, *Lady Huntingdon and Her Correspondence*, 104.
[13] Cook, *Countess of Huntingdon*, 216.

9
Drawing-Room Evangelism

"Fill her place while she felt the Lord with her," Howell Harris had advised Selina Hastings during her period of mourning. In an atmosphere of loss, the bereaved widow was tempted to withdraw from the world to a life of solitude, supposing that this was the way to unbroken communion with God.[1] For a time she turned to the writings of the mystics. Selina's earlier letters to Charles Wesley uncover a heavy reliance on feelings and subjective experience as an expression of her faith. The danger of mysticism is the relegation of Scripture to a lesser guide in the spiritual life; emotions certainly have a part to play but never ought to displace the former. This was why it was enough of a concern for Harris to mention the matter in a letter to George Whitefield in 1747.[2] The company of faithful servants of Christ with joint fervor for evangelism providentially helped to draw Selina away from plunging too deeply into mystical thinking. It was not long before her inclination to flee public life was overcome by her passion to pursue lost souls.

Spurred to action, Lady Huntingdon deliberated on her next move. Preaching in the open-air, Whitefield and the Wesleys had begun a gospel ministry to the masses—but how were they to evangelize to the nobility for whom it was inconceivable to associate with such a group as the Methodists much less stand in their midst? The Countess would leverage her position of privilege and influence to reach them. As a peeress of the realm, she was legally permitted to appoint private chaplains to tend to the spiritual

---

[1] Harding, *Selina, Countess of Huntingdon*, 41.

[2] *Selected Trevecca Letters*, 2:11 (17 December 1747), quoted in Cook, *Countess of Huntingdon*, 107.

needs of her household; guests dining and being entertained at her home, she envisioned, could benefit from this arrangement. The one to do it, she believed, was George Whitefield who had already gained celebrity status throughout England for his preaching. Combine this with the persuasive solicitations of a high-ranking aristocrat and no doubt there were to be obliged and intent, if not curious, hearers. From the fields, then, the gospel was now to go to the drawing-rooms of the Countess of Huntingdon's estates.

Whitefield had left again for America in 1744, but upon his return in 1748 he received the Countess' invitation to preach at her Chelsea home in London. He was sincerely humbled, "I am ashamed to think your Ladyship will admit me under your roof," yet nonetheless enlivened by the prospects of such a ministry:

> I write this to inform your Ladyship that I am quite willing to comply with your invitation ... Blessed be God, that the rich and great begin to have an hearing ear. I think it is a good sign that our Lord intends to give to some at least, an obedient heart. Surely your Ladyship [is] only the [firstfruit]. May you increase and multiply! I believe you will. How wonderfully does our Redeemer deal with souls. If they will hear the gospel only under a ceiled roof, ministers shall be sent to them there ... "Paul preached privately to those that were of reputation." This must be the way I presume of dealing with the nobility, who yet know not the Lord. O that I may be enabled, when called to preach to any of them, so to preach as to win their souls to the blessed Jesus![3]

In September Whitefield wrote a letter expressing his gratitude to Lady Huntingdon for making him one of her chaplains,[4] a decision that most explicitly showed her assent to the Calvinist position.[5]

---

[3] Tyson, *Lady Huntingdon and Her Correspondence*, 73, August 21, 1748.
[4] Tyson, *Lady Huntingdon and Her Correspondence*, 74, September 1, 1748.
[5] Dallimore, *George Whitefield*, 157.

Drawing-Room Evangelism

Considering the possibilities that could open up for a minister when backed by a Countess with substantial connections, the appointment must not have been easy for the Wesleys, especially John, to accept. Still John preached in Whitefield's place whenever he was away, even while feeling unenthused about doing the bidding of the nobility (just as he had been less than pleased when his brother had a seat reserved for the Countess at the Foundery that could only be given up in her absence).[6] Perhaps coming from a more modest upbringing, Whitefield was understandably apprehensive about preaching before such prominent men and women, among them politicians, philosophers, poets, army generals, even royalty: "I go with fear and trembling, knowing how difficult it is to speak to the great so as to win them to Jesus Christ. But divine grace is sufficient for me."[7] Pride, vanity, and ease were natural barriers for the well-to-do; but Whitefield—looking past the extravagantly dressed, their polished manners and conversations—saw the unconverted desperately needing to hear the humbling message of the gospel. Remember the Duchess of Buckingham's earlier revulsion when told that she had a heart as sinful as the common man—the cutting truth is that sin does not discriminate based on rank, and so Whitefield preached to lost souls in need of faith in a Redeemer.

Responses were varied. Some were amazed by Whitefield's skill but never converted, such as Lord Bolingbroke and the Earl of Chesterfield. Bolingbroke could nevertheless request to see Whitefield again (even offering some money to support his Georgia orphanage), while Chesterfield lauded the preacher, "Mr Whitefield's eloquence is unrivalled—his zeal inexhaustible; and not to admire both would argue a total absence of taste."[8] Soon Whitefield was preaching twice a week on the Countess' estate

---

[6] Cook, *Countess of Huntingdon*, 88–89.

[7] Dallimore, *George Whitefield*, 159.

[8] *Whitefield: Life and Times*, 269, quoted in Dallimore, *George Whitefield*, 160.

The Bold Evangelist

and his popularity with the crowd prompted her to lease another property on Park Street to provide a better situated setting for his preaching. Whitefield, receiving such accolades, was wary of the compulsion to swell with self-importance, writing to a friend, "Who knows what God may do? He can never work by a meaner instrument. I want humility, I want thankfulness, I want a heart continually flaming with the love of God."[9] The nobles who did convert demonstrated the authenticity of their faith upon enduring ridicule and judgment just as Lady Huntingdon had. One of them was Selina's aunt, the enchanting Lady Frances Shirley (who had once stolen the affections of Chesterfield).[10] Never himself embracing the gospel, Chesterfield was not an impediment to the gospel reaching his family: his own sister Lady Gertrude Hotham converted, and so did his wife Lady Chesterfield and her sister the Countess Delitz. In fact the Countess' ministry was later emulated by some of these ladies who opened up their own homes for preaching.[11] Reputed statesmen like the Earl of Bath and Lord Dartmouth not only converted but used their standing for the Christian cause.[12]

If the outcome of the Countess of Huntingdon's drawing-room ministry were measured solely by numbers converted, we would easily deem it negligible, writing it off as well-intentioned but unsuccessful in light of her more far-reaching missionary endeavours. We ought to remember the Countess' earlier question "What if you save but one soul?" that she pressed upon John Wesley; Selina was not simply driven by the project but the person. Certainly she had hoped that the ministry would have resulted in a greater portion of the leading figures converting, thereby fulfilling her desire for England's religious reform. This

---

[9] Whitefield, *Works*, 2:221, quoted in Cook, *Countess of Huntingdon*, 119.
[10] Cook, *Countess of Huntingdon*, 120–121.
[11] Cook, *Countess of Huntingdon*, 122–123.
[12] Cook, *Countess of Huntingdon*, 124–125.

Drawing-Room Evangelism

was evident in her plan to bring Methodism to Frederick, the Prince of Wales, who was next in line for the throne. Although this was never realized (he died in 1751), his esteem of the Countess must be duly noted. Once in court when his asking about the whereabouts of the Countess provoked a noble to sarcastically remark that she was likely praying with her beggars, the Prince defended the Countess: "When I am dying I think I shall be happy to seize the skirt of Lady Huntingdon's mantle to lift me up with her to heaven."[13] The prince's response reflects the vital contribution of the Countess' drawing-room ministry to the Revival: it helped to moderate the disparaging opinions of the upper class toward the Methodists.[14] The fullness of its effects may not be known, but credit must be given to this stage of Lady Huntingdon's evangelistic ministry.

The Methodist movement entering the 1750s was widening its influence and taking discernible form. Its representatives were fulfilling their designated roles while doing what was in their capacity to support their co-labourers. Many other ministers would come to preach in the Countess' drawing rooms, including William Romaine, Martin Madan (1726–1790), and Henry Venn (1725–1797). The Countess' skill in presenting a compelling case for her mission to the nobility explains the willingness of these preachers to support her, as seen in a letter from a humble John Fletcher to Charles Wesley in 1759:

> Charity, politeness, and reason accompanied [the Countess'] offer; and I confess, in spite of the resolution which it had almost absolutely formed, to fly the houses of the great, without even the exception of the Countess', I found myself so greatly changed that I should have accepted, on the spot, a proposal which I should have declined from any other

---

[13] Cook, *Countess of Huntingdon*, 127.
[14] Cook, *Countess of Huntingdon*, 128.

mouth ... when I had reflected on her obliging offer, I would do myself the honour of waiting upon her again. ... Can I accept an office for which I have such small talents? And shall I not dishonour the cause of God, by stammering out the mysteries of the Gospel in a place where the most approved ministers of the Lord have preached with so much power and so much success?[15]

Underneath the clashes between Methodist parties was a longing for peace so that the fruits of the Revival would continue. Already at the onset of his ministry to the aristocracy, Whitefield—beholding his obligations to those in Britain and America—had realized that his greatest burden was to do the work of evangelism and thus came to the decision to relinquish his leadership of the Calvinistic Methodists.[16] In so doing, he also freed him and John Wesley from relentless disputes over their theological differences. The grand task of overseeing the Methodist societies went to John whose gift of administration had already been proven. Yielding to what he was sure was his divine call, Whitefield also expressed his recognition of the Countess', writing to her at the end of 1753:

> Few have either courage or conduct to head a Christian party amongst persons of high life. That honour seems to be put upon your Ladyship:—and a glorious honour indeed it is ... I pray the Lord of all lords to lengthen out your important life, and make your Ladyship ten thousand times more useful than ever, long after my worthless head is laid in the silent grave.[17]

Selina's home—once drawing guests that relished in delectable meals and courtly chatter—had become far more than just that. The Countess of Huntingdon focused less on her riches and

---

[15] Tyson, *Lady Huntingdon and Her Correspondence*, 130.
[16] Dallimore, *George Whitefield*, 65.
[17] Tyson, *Lady Huntingdon and Her Correspondence*, 79–80.

Drawing-Room Evangelism

more on the riches of her salvation in Jesus Christ. Beyond the grandeur of a mansion, her home had become a setting for evangelism, and even further, a setting for Christian fellowship. In a letter to the recently converted Countess Delitz, Whitefield presents a moving picture of Selina and the godly activities filling her home:

> Good Lady Huntingdon goes on acting the part of a mother in Israel, more and more. For a day or two she has had five clergymen under her roof, which makes her Ladyship look like a good Archbishop with his chaplains around him. Her house is indeed a Bethel. To us in the ministry, it looks like a college. We have the sacrament every morning, heavenly conversation all day, and preach at night. This is to live at Court, indeed.[18]

Selina understood well the truth of Whitefield's words: Court was "where Jesus reigns," he wrote to her, "where he has erected a spiritual kingdom in the heart. All besides this, is only tinsel and glitter. Here alone is real and abiding happiness to be found."

---

[18] Tyson, *Lady Huntingdon and Her Correspondence*, 75.

10
The Countess' Chapels

As a loyal member of the Church of England the Countess of Huntingdon had never intended to separate from it. Her aim had been to revive the religious life of the state church from within. Societies were set up to nurture the spiritual growth of converts but were encouraged to attend their local parishes for official services and to receive communion. This remained the purpose when the Countess' early chapels were set up. Already seen was her resolve to use whatever resources she could to meet the spiritual needs of hearers; when hurdles emerged that threatened to obstruct her goal of evangelism, Selina, always the woman of action, promptly took counteractive measures.

Methodist Leaders Refused Ordination
The first hurdle was not being able to find bishops who were willing to ordain evangelical leaders in the Revival. Recall Bishop Martin Benson's regret over ordaining George Whitefield because of his field preaching. Bishops were increasingly refusing to ordain individuals with Methodist leanings out of fear that they would bring disorder into the church. They could not recognize that their zeal was a reflection of true conversion, a powerful work of God in the sinner's heart sparking eagerness to proclaim it. At this point Lady Huntingdon was still trying to take advantage of her existing connections with bishops to gain ordination for Methodists. These connections derived from either earlier friendships or contacts made with bishops during her health visits to Bath. They were few, however, and the situation would grow dim in the

1770s upon the deaths of those bishops who stood a chance of helping her.¹

Methodists Dissatisfied with Local Parish Churches

The second hurdle was that even though individuals converting during the Revival were urged to attend services at their local parish churches, they were not always well-received. For one, they were denied participation in Holy Communion. While Methodists like Lady Huntingdon and the Wesleys were adamant about upholding their allegiance to the Church of England, others were not so thoroughly convinced, restless with and resistant of the formalities imposed on them. Those who were completely dissatisfied ultimately removed themselves from the church's grasp, exercising their freedom within the boundaries of the Toleration Act. Enacted in 1689 following the Glorious Revolution, the Toleration Act made allowance for congregations that registered themselves as Dissenting meeting places. Dissenters still faced discrimination (they were barred from attending the nation's universities and being involved in England's civil and political life), but at least by identifying themselves as such they secured some freedom in how they worshipped. This was precisely what Whitefield was forced to do when he failed to license his meeting house on Tottenham Court Road. In 1756 he reported to Lady Huntingdon the response he received from the House of Commons, illustrating the challenges the Methodists faced in trying to procure proper venues for worship:

> No nobleman can licence a chapel, or in any manner have one put in his dwelling house; that the chapel must be a private one, and not with doors to the street for any persons to resort to at pleasure, for then it becomes a public one; that a chapel cannot be built and used as such, without the

---

[1] Welch, *Spiritual Pilgrim*, 95.

The Countess' Chapels

consent of the parson of the parish, and when it is done with his consent, no minister can preach therein, without licence of the Bishop of the diocese.[2]

The Countess' Solution

Selina's predicament was that she had no desire to resort to Dissent like some of her Methodist cohorts, yet the Church of England still posed limitations on her evangelism. Given that many evangelicals turned to Dissent as a way of escaping these constraints, how did Selina escape without doing the same? The solution once again lay in her privilege as peeress of the realm: legally the Countess was allowed to have a chapel attached to her home for the spiritual ministering of her household. Outsiders, according to the law, were permitted to attend services at the chapel. In effect, through her chapels the Countess seemed to be creating an extension of her drawing room. For more than two decades she exploited this loophole, chapel services taking place whether she was on her estate or not.

The building of all her chapels was made feasible through different means—money was borrowed, an existing structure was leased, a contribution was made by a collaborator, or the Countess funded the project herself. Thomas Haweis described the generosity of his patroness:

> Never perhaps did mortal make nobler use of what she possessed, live less attached to earth or dispense it with more open hand. I have often said she was one of the poor who lived upon her own bounty ... I leave this testimony to her worth in this respect, that every shilling she possessed should be employed for the glory of God. But with all her fortune and self-denial her finances were inadequate to her calls, and it was impossible that she could have done the

---

[2] Tyson, *Lady Huntingdon and Her Correspondence*, 97-98, June 4, 1756.

noble acts that marked her character if she had not found such men as these with disinterested zeal.³

Each chapel that was built and the fruitful ministry that ensued inspired Lady Huntingdon to build another, so that by the end of her life as many as 64 chapels were registered under her name. Sketches from this period of chapel-building reveal the impressive scale of this ministry.

Brighton Chapel, 1761
Like Bath, Brighton was becoming a popular tourist area for the affluent. The town's main attraction was sea bathing. In 1758 Selina had brought her ill son Henry there. During her stay she met a group of women desiring to study the Scriptures, which naturally led to the establishment of a religious society. With the influx of people coming in to Brighton, places available for worship were lacking. Lady Huntingdon saw the need and acted, writing to Charles Wesley in August 1758: "I seem to stand upon that desert that the promise is made to: 'I will open a way in the wilderness and a high way in the desert' [Is. 43:19], and here I wait to see His hand doing both for me."⁴ The Countess borrowed 500 pounds from Lady Gertrude Hotham, but still facing insufficient funds, she sold more than that amount in jewels to fund the remainder of the project.⁵ The Brighton Chapel, an initiative that was entirely the Countess' idea, showed the freedom and independence she was able to exercise in widowhood.

The chapel opened in June of that year and Martin Madan (for whom she secured ordination) preached the sermon. Other preachers who assisted in the Brighton ministry included William Romaine, John Fletcher, John Berridge, and Henry Venn. Most of

---

³ Cook, *Countess of Huntingdon*, 199–200.
⁴ Tyson, *Lady Huntingdon and Her Correspondence*, 101.
⁵ Welch, *Spiritual Pilgrim*, 99.

The Countess' Chapels

these clergymen oversaw their own congregations but travelled to Brighton whenever they could to assist her. The congregation grew at such an amazing rate that in 1767 the Countess added an extension to the chapel.[6] Witnessing the spiritual fruit born by this body of believers, she called for a day of prayer before its reopening, a time for everyone to praise the Lord for his mighty provision and to recommit their labors to God. Emboldened by what he saw of this congregation, Berridge wrote a letter of support to the Countess: "Go on, my dear lady, build and fight manfully, and believe lustily. Look upwards and press forwards. Heaven's eternal hills are before you."[7]

Ote Hall Chapel, 1762
Build, Selina did. Not long after the first chapel was built in Brighton, Ote Hall was opened near Wivelsfield, Sussex, eight miles from Brighton. The project was made possible by a distant Shirley relative who offered to lease the home, whose hall was converted to a place for worship. William Romaine devoted much time tending to this congregation since he was one of the few clergymen not tied down by his own flock (disapproval of his popular evangelical preaching led to his dismissal from his St George congregation in 1755). Learning about his situation, Lady Huntingdon invited Romaine to preach at her Park Street home, and in 1761 he became her chaplain. It was also during this time that the Countess' daughter Lady Selina had passed away, and the Countess' temporary leave had put a halt to the ministry at Ote Hall.[8] Having earlier witnessed the pleas of John Berridge and John Fletcher to resume her labor, we come to recognize just how indispensable her service was—for it was the Countess who assumed the entire administrative responsibility of ensuring the pulpits at her chapels

---

[6] Welch, *Spiritual Pilgrim*, 99.
[7] Tyson, *Lady Huntingdon and Her Correspondence*, 159.
[8] Cook, *Countess of Huntingdon*, 214–216.

were filled. Without her requests, even demands, in letters to clergymen to preach at her chapels, the enterprise risked breaking down. This is pictured in Berridge's lighthearted letter to Lady Huntingdon in July 1763 explaining his whereabouts and acknowledging her displeasure with his delay in arriving at Ote Hall:

> I will not inform you where I lodge in town, but I should have another letter from Ote Hall to heat up my quarters. Do now let me preach quietly in [London] for two days, and you may scold me for it afterwards, if you will. But I must inform you, that I am mighty apt to laugh when a scolding is over, especially if it be performed without ill-nature.[9]

No doubt to lift the Countess' spirits following her daughter's death, Lord Dartmouth encouraged her with these words: "You will be rewarded openly before an assembled world, when we shall swell that innumerable train of children which the Lord hath given to you."[10] When the ministry at Ote Hall did resume, it yielded a remarkable harvest.

Bretby Hall Chapel, 1765

Although the gospel had not taken root in the heart of Lord Chesterfield, his high regard for George Whitefield nonetheless inspired him to open his estate for Methodist preaching. His mansion sat in a beautifully-wooded area of Derbyshire and guests were led to his chapel at Bretby Hall.[11] Romaine described the ministry taking place here: "Showers of grace came down; sinners in great numbers were awakened, and believers comforted."[12]

---

[9] Tyson, *Lady Huntingdon and Her Correspondence*, 131.

[10] Seymour, *Selina Countess of Huntingdon*, 1:335, quoted in Cook, *Countess of Huntingdon*, 215.

[11] Cook, *Countess of Huntingdon*, 223.

[12] Robert Philip, *The Life and Times of the Reverend George Whitefield* (London: 1838), 513.

The Countess' Chapels

Those that came to listen to Whitefield's preaching numbered so many that services had to be relocated to Bretby Park.

Bath Chapel, 1765

It was Bath's curative hot springs that had first brought Lady Huntingdon here, reluctant as she was, but now she beheld opportunity. In 1764, in an area known as the Vineyards, construction began for the Bath chapel, which offered a panoramic view of the countryside. Desiring to appeal to the refined palates of neighboring aristocrats, the Countess invested careful consideration into its aesthetics.[13] During its construction, however, she wrote to Charles Wesley of her dismay over receiving no public support for the project:

> My chapel is above ground, and I find I am heartily wished die before it is finished. I am sure of your prayers for its success, but I think it is remarkable that I have not had a line from one creature to rejoice in its being built; but by that and all things else it is a matter quite between my heart and our only best friend, and that being sufficient I can want no more.[14]

Relying not on the estimations of men, Selina pressed on. When construction was finally complete, the grand opening of the Bath chapel in the fall of 1765 drew many, some out of sincere spiritual interest, others out of sheer curiosity. Lady Huntingdon did not want to miss out on the prospect of reaching such a large crowd and summoned as many Methodist leaders as she could to preach. It was also during this period that she compiled 231 hymns to be sung at her chapels.[15] The collection included such noteworthy hymn-writers as Isaac Watts, Charles Wesley, Philip Doddridge,

---

[13] Cook, *Countess of Huntingdon*, 222.
[14] Tyson, *Lady Huntingdon and Her Correspondence*, 106.
[15] Cook, *Countess of Huntingdon*, 230.

John Newton, William Cowper, Augustus Toplady, Walter Shirley, and Anne Steele, some as we have seen were her dear friends.

Tunbridge Wells, 1769
This region was yet another beautiful spa town that drew the nobility. In the spring of 1768, at her own expense the Countess purchased a property in Mount Ephraim and expressed to Whitefield in April of her assurance in its resultant fruit which she had already witnessed in her other chapels: "Great will be the work in this place."[16] Whitefield preached at the chapel's opening services, among the final services he would conduct for the Countess before making his last trip to America in the early fall. Listening to the sweet hymn-singing of the attendees and seeing the tears of convicted hearts, Selina must have felt renewed, understandably worn by the demands of sustaining her chapel-ministry.[17] In the same letter to Whitefield, she called attention to her difficulty in securing preachers for her pulpits: "Mr. Venn cannot be at Bath; [Cradock] Glascott must supply but Sussex. Alas! I know not how the Lord will provide but sure I am it will."[18]

A Growing Need for Preachers
And there were numerous chapels to provide for, the ones in Brighton, Bath, and Tunbridge Wells simply occupied the most popular districts; there were others—the Norwich Chapel in 1755, Lewes Chapel in 1765, Ewer Street Chapel in 1770, Paradise Street Chapel in 1774, Swansea Chapel in 1789—and the list goes on. As more and more chapels were set up, the pressure to find able, willing, and available preachers intensified, with only about

---

[16] Tyson, *Lady Huntingdon and Her Correspondence*, 109.
[17] Cook, *Countess of Huntingdon*, 248, 258.
[18] Tyson, *Lady Huntingdon and Her Correspondence*, 109.

The Countess' Chapels

twenty clergymen she could access for support.[19] Her preachers were pulled by the need to assist in her bourgeoning ministry as well as the duty to serve in their own. It was not always possible for a minister to find a substitute in his absence. Add to this the taxing journey back and forth between congregations. Not surprisingly, Lady Huntingdon could be very assertive in sending for a preacher, and a graver letter from Berridge shows the reality of her situation:

> I am not well able to ride so long a journey; and my heart is utterly set against wheel-carriages on these roads. Indeed I see not my call; I cannot think of the journey; and therefore pray your ladyship to think no more of it. I write plainly, not out of forwardness, I trust, but to save your ladyship the trouble of sending a second request, and myself the pain of returning a second denial.[20]

The 1760s in the Countess of Huntingdon's ministry bore witness to vast numbers transformed by the Spirit of God. It also saw many new preachers entering into the Countess' network. Yet the obvious need remained: it was impractical for her to shoulder the entire burden of ensuring that chapels were looked after and that faithful evangelical preachers were assuming their pulpits. After hearing from Charles Wesley about the progress in Bath, she felt the need even more: "Your kind account of Bath revives me. I believe the Lord has many to call there and with such a thirst for the preaching that is quite distressing while so few laborers are yet in the vineyard."[21] Thus began the next phase in the life of Selina Hastings, the founding of Trevecca College.

---

[19] Harding, *Selina, Countess of Huntingdon*, 73.
[20] Cook, *Countess of Huntingdon*, 198.
[21] Tyson, *Lady Huntingdon and Her Correspondence*, 110.

11
Trevecca College

Setting up chapels was one task, but supplying preachers to assume their pulpits was another. The resourcefulness and determination of the Countess led to their establishment and her gift of organization enabled her to manage them, yet without accessibility to preachers, the enterprise would suffer. When no one was available to supply the need, a pulpit was shut down.

The idea to erect an institution that would provide training for prospective ministers had occurred to the Countess years earlier. The complications she was now facing caused her to revisit the idea and fortified her resolve to undertake the venture. There were also other factors that created the need for such a college. The Methodist movement saw not only the multiplying of converts but also the potential or desire of some to enter into the ministry. But the atmosphere proved limiting. These individuals, already facing the barrier to ordination because bishops were skeptical of their evangelical convictions, were at a disadvantage because ordination in the Church of England typically necessitated a university education, which meant opportunities were closed to those who did not possess formal academic training or lacked the financial means to obtain it.

Persecution of Methodist Students at Oxford University
The problem was most pronounced when in March 1768 six students were expelled from Oxford University for their Methodist views. While plans for Trevecca were already underway, the event reinforced the need for a college geared specifically for evangelicals.

The Bold Evangelist

The principal at Oxford, Dr. George Dixon, and the vice-principal, Dr. John Higson, were in disagreement with each other regarding the Methodists. Dixon accepted and defended the students while Higson indignantly opposed them. The latter went as far as launching a formal complaint to the university's Vice-Chancellor, criticizing the students for their inadequate educational background, and more seriously, their unlawful ministerial activities—taking their own initiatives in preaching, praying, reading Scripture and gathering in homes to sing hymns—all the while unordained.[1] The students, labeled "Enthusiasts," were perceived as opponents of the Established Church.

A trial ensued following Higson's complaint but the case was blatantly one-sided and ultimately led to the expulsion of the students. The university and the Church, exposed by the controversy, drew the attention of the press. Everyone knew about the outcome of the trial, including Lady Huntingdon. Reports, objective or not, featured both sides of the heated debate which concerned the unfair treatment of the students. That spring George Whitefield wrote a letter directly to the Vice-Chancellor defending the character and actions of the students.[2] The Countess herself approached the students and offered to provide for their education, and two of the students eventually enrolled at her college.[3]

Plans for Trevecca College

The Countess was not the only one with a vision of establishing a centre for equipping future evangelical ministers. John Wesley had considered it for his Kingswood school in Bristol in the late 1740s, and observations were made that his later criticism of the Countess' new venture stemmed from his jealousy.[4] Howell

---

[1] Cook, *Countess of Huntingdon*, 244.
[2] Cook, *Countess of Huntingdon*, 245.
[3] Cook, *Countess of Huntingdon*, 248.
[4] Luke Tyerman, *Wesley*, 3:35, quoted in Cook, *Countess of Huntingdon*, 250.

Trevecca College

Harris had spoken of the same vision two decades earlier and upon sharing it with the Countess in the early 1760s the two became collaborators. Known today as College Farm, Trefeca Isaf, an old building Harris was renting from his brother in South Wales, became the site for the college. The location had its advantages. Its proximity to Harris's home meant that the Welshman could oversee the construction and operation of the college.[5] The tranquil countryside offered favorable conditions for young men needing to flee the temptations of city life to nurture their spiritual lives and concentrate on their studies.

To fill the position of President at Trevecca College, the Countess asked John Fletcher. The vicar of Madeley offered a wholehearted response to her invitation:

> With regard to the superintendency of the College, or the examination of the candidates, I know myself too well to dream about it; nevertheless, so far as my present calling and poor abilities will allow, I am ready to throw in my mite into the treasury.[6]

The fact that Lady Huntingdon, a Calvinist, requested Fletcher, an Arminian, to take charge of the college is evidence that her vision at the outset was to provide training for faithful converts showing promise in serving the Methodist movement at large and that theological differences was not a divisive factor.

A description in 1775 of Trevecca College is provided by an outside observer who was not at all supportive of the Methodist cause:

> The House, modern gothic, stands in a pleasant spot, about 3 ½ miles out off the Road ... [The students] were about 20

---

[5] Cook, *Countess of Huntingdon*, 234.
[6] Tyson, *Lady Huntingdon and Her Correspondence*, 160.

The Bold Evangelist

years of age, dressed chiefly in black, very grave and attentive to their business. Their Master was a decent man, about 30 years of age. The Schoolroom is a very pleasant Apartment with a Collection of Books in it ... The Chapel is a neat pretty room. A handsome Eating Room, used when her Ladyship is among them, for thither she sometimes comes, and makes a short Residence. The Common Eating Room is small. The Walls of the whole House are adorned with Scripture Passages, and that selected over the Chimney in the Eating Room is, 'Feed my Sheep.' Her Ladyship's Apartment is very small, but the whole is extremely neat, and all the Rooms cheerful, calculated to improve much more lively and pleasant sentiments than seemed to reign there.[7]

The Opening of Trevecca College

The grand opening took place on the Countess of Huntingdon's sixty-first birthday on 24 August 1768. Fifteen students were enrolled at the time.[8] Whitefield preached at the ceremony and the days following. A number of Methodist leaders and a large congregation were in attendance. The extensive project that took years to be realized culminated in a joyous celebration. Fletcher could testify to the unity and excitement of the surroundings and was heartened by what was to come. He left the college to tend to his other responsibilities in Madeley and in the Revival; upon his return a few months later, however, he noticed that the initial spiritual vigor had abated. On the same day that Fletcher protested to the Countess about his displeasure with the students' lackadaisical attitudes, he pulled each one aside and reprimanded him.[9]

Fletcher was driven by his desire to see to the growth of these future ministers of the gospel, longing for a "love for prayer, an end of divisions and a degree of zeal for God and brotherly

---

[7] Welch, *Spiritual Pilgrim*, 117.
[8] Cook, *Countess of Huntingdon*, 252.
[9] Cook, *Countess of Huntingdon*, 255.

Trevecca College

kindness, watchfulness and an apparent concern for souls."[10] In the years following, the students would testify to how much they benefitted from the direction of this God-fearing leader. His words that day had so affected the students that a couple of them were moved to break from the usual proceedings to recommit themselves to the divine call.[11] The break was spent in prayer, fasting, confession, and hymn-singing. Lady Huntingdon was greatly encouraged by the unraveling of events. While the years ahead were not without problems, her desire for the students, along with that of the other Methodist leaders who offered their hand in training and preaching (among them Charles Wesley, William Williams of Pantycelyn, Daniel Rowland, and John Berridge), reverberated throughout the college: "O for a day of power on these young men there; may free grace so overpower their own souls as to preach salvation gloriously and freely to every sinner they meet!"[12]

Trevecca College Up-Close

Students that were considered for enrollment at Trevecca rested on the recommendations of the Countess' trusted friends and ministers. Individuals that showed potential were recognized by their character and spiritual earnestness, aptitude for learning, and capacity to fulfill her need for itinerary preachers. When asked about prospective students, Fletcher wrote to the Countess about the challenge of finding faithful laborers for Christ: "Our Israel is small, my Lady, and if among 600 hundred thousand, only two faithful men were found of old, the Joshuas and Calebs cannot be numerous among us."[13] Yet, that evening, when he had gone

---

[10] Cook, *Countess of Huntingdon*, 256.
[11] Cook, *Countess of Huntingdon*, 255.
[12] *Selected Trevecka Letters*, 2:133-134, quoted in Cook, *Countess of Huntingdon*, 260.
[13] Tyson, *Lady Huntingdon and Her Correspondence*, 160.

The Bold Evangelist

to bed, a young man by the name of James Glazebrook appeared in his dream, which later prompted Fletcher to recall a conversation Glazebrook had with him regarding feeling the call to become a preacher, a longing, Glazebrook said, that had been with him for four years. Moved by the dream, Fletcher wanted to find and speak to Glazebrook at once, only to find that he had come to see Fletcher in Madeley that very morning.[14] Not long after Glazebrook enrolled at Trevecca. For the next 23 years until the Countess' death, over two hundred men would pass through the college.[15]

As for the books that students were to be immersed in, a running list of suggestions was provided by Fletcher. Having studied in Geneva, he urged the Countess to also consult others whom he considered more informed than he regarding the "best" and most "concise" English books (he referred her to Joseph Townsend and Charles Wesley). Fletcher believed that essential to the program was "Grammar, Logic, Rhetoric, with Ecclesiastical History, and a little Natural Philosophy, and Geography, with a great deal of practical divinity." A sample may prove to be instructive even for the twenty-first century reader:

> Watt's *Logic*, and his *History of the Bible by Questions and Answers*, which seem to me excellent books of the kind for clearness and order. Mr. Wesley's *Natural Philosophy* contains as much as is wanted, or more. Mason's *Essay on Pronunciation* will be worth their attention. [Matthew] Henry and Gill on the Bible, with the four volumes of [Richard] Baxter's *Practical Works*, Keach's *Metaphors*, Taylor on the *Types* (printed at Trevecca), Gurnal's *Christian Armour*, Edwards on *Preaching*, Johnson's *English Dictionary*, and

---

[14] Cook, *Countess of Huntingdon*, 236.
[15] Harding, *Selina Countess of Huntingdon*, 170.

Trevecca College

Mr. Wesley's *Christian Library*, may make part of the little library.[16]

The same could be said for the spiritual exercises that the students were required to complete. For entry into the college, some were asked to give a thorough answer to the question, "What is faith?" using the Bible as their only source. As for their studies, below is a sampling of the assignments prepared by Fletcher, which reveals the academic and, even more importantly, theological standards set for the students at Trevecca:

> Write an English letter to a Deist to convince him of the truth of the Scriptures.
> Make an English theme upon the mischief of unsanctified learning.
> Draw up an address to Jesus for the gift of the Holy Ghost, urging the strongest reasons you can think of to engage him to grant it to you.
> Try in a letter to convince one who has not the spiritual kingdom set up in his soul that he never had the true Christian faith or is backslidden.[17]

The schedule at Trevecca was rigid and the students were under close supervision (not surprising with someone like Lady Huntingdon as overseer). The students were expected to rise by five in the morning and assemble for worship at six; arriving all neat and tidy in their uniforms, the students would often find the Countess already waiting for them.[18] The weekends were designated for preaching; students were sent out to various locations to fulfill pulpit demands, all of which were arranged by the Countess

---

[16] Cook, *Countess of Huntingdon*, 238.
[17] Cook, *Countess of Huntingdon*, 262.
[18] Cook, *Countess of Huntingdon*, 301–302.

herself. When the weekend was out, the students were to return and resume their studies.

Challenges at Trevecca College

For such a grand undertaking, problems were bound to surface, and for Trevecca, a training college and seminary that was the first of its kind, even more so. The circumstances began to pose problems for the students. Remember that setting up the college arose from the Countess' need to supply preachers for her pulpits, so very often the impulse was to settle this need, which dictated what was on the students' agenda. What inevitably happened was that the students' academics suffered, and paradoxically, the more a student showed potential, the likelier he was sent out more frequently and for longer periods. It was understandable that the students who genuinely wanted to be engaged in their studies expressed their frustration to the Countess. One student eventually left the college; another reasoned with her, "although learning does not make ministers, it is necessary for ministers to have it that they may be able to vindicate the truths of God."[19] At the same time the reverse situation took place: after visiting and preaching to a congregation for a short time, a student would witness the fruit born by his ministry and the relationships nurtured and felt reluctant to leave it. Longing to continue God's work in fostering its growth, he would plead with the Countess to let him stay with the same congregation for longer (rather than being relocated to another congregation that needed a preacher).[20]

In both cases, however, the Countess was not likely to yield to the students' wishes. Since she was responsible for all the expenses associated with the college, it seemed reasonable to her to expect the students to comply with her wishes.[21] The Countess

---

[19] Cook, *Countess of Huntingdon*, 312.
[20] Cook, *Countess of Huntingdon*, 312-313.
[21] Cook, *Countess of Huntingdon*, 313.

Trevecca College

assumed the cost of their entire education, from their living accommodations down to their food and clothing. If discovering that a student was negligent or irresponsible with his spending, she acted sensibly, urging him to exercise greater vigilance with her financial provisions. Likewise when a student was perceived to be uncooperative with her requests, she did not hesitate to exert her authority over the individual. When we evaluate her actions, Faith Cook's biography offers a sympathetic defense, reminding us to consider what was at stake for her:

> The Countess did not minimize the importance of a well-educated ministry, nor depreciate learning, but with vast tracts of the countryside still untouched by the Christian gospel, and congregations urging her to send a student to supply their churches, she felt she must balance one urgency against the other.[22]

Lady Huntingdon's Devotion to the Students

Challenges aside, the Countess' love for the students at Trevecca was sure. John Wesley, though not writing from a supportive spirit, had observed: "Trevecca is much more to Lady Huntingdon than Kingswood is to me."[23] Wesley's words point to the Countess' deep and visible bond with her students. Her care for these young, promising laborers of God included their physical, emotional and spiritual wellbeing.

Though she was prudent with how money was spent at the college, she nevertheless sought to ensure that the students were sufficiently provided for as she wrote to one student in 1774:

> Could your clothes do tolerably, till this very bad weather is a little over, it would be well. I know you are so clean and careful. I can never wish you to have less; but new clothes

---

[22] Cook, *Countess of Huntingdon*, 312.
[23] Cook, *Countess of Huntingdon*, 266.

to ride in must so soon be spoiled at this season, that I will leave it with you to judge; and when you see fit, order them, and send me the bill.[24]

In 1771 another student Joseph Shipman (one of the students expelled from Oxford) fell gravely ill, so Lady Huntingdon directed him to Bristol in hopes that the therapeutic waters could help; when his condition worsened, she directed him to his one and only source of hope—Jesus Christ—whose atoning work on the Cross could triumph over all weakness, fear, and doubt: "Keep this point in the darkest hour, He died ... This truth the great enemy of our souls can never attack."[25] Months later Shipman passed away but proclaimed just before his final hour of his full assurance that he was to meet his God.

When one student became discouraged by his efforts at Trevecca, feeling that he could not meet the college's rigorous demands, rather than sternness Lady Huntingdon responded with gentleness to reassure him. Most of these men, upon enrolling at the college, were inexperienced in the world of preaching, yet speaking at the funeral of the Countess many years later a former Trevecca student fondly recalled his early trepidation of the crowd and how he found consolation in the remembrance of the Countess' prodding words: "You are only going to a few simple souls; tell them concerning Jesus Christ and they will be satisfied."[26]

The warmest picture of all is summed up by the students' testimonies of the Countess' spiritual dealings with them. It was evident that her love was profoundly felt by many:

---

[24] Cook, *Countess of Huntingdon*, 310.
[25] Cook, *Countess of Huntingdon*, 305.
[26] Cook, *Countess of Huntingdon*, 307.

Trevecca College

> Her Ladyship is such a woman that nobody can refuse anything that she asks. She is a mother to us all and indeed she calls us her children. She takes so many of us into her room every night and makes us read a chapter [of Scripture] to her, and she explains it to us and there is few ministers could do it better and she prays with us.[27]

And from another student:

> She regarded her young men as her sons, as her family. With what affection and tenderness, wisdom and prudence have I heard her address the young men in the study around her. How has she warned, cautioned, reproved, comforted and encouraged us as she saw cause like a true mother in Israel. With what earnest, feeling, melting prayers has she poured out her soul to God among us. The simplicity with which she would express herself, the variety of her petitions, accompanied with many tears running down her aged cheeks had dissolved all about her into a flood of weeping.[28]

Even while juggling her multitude of responsibilities in the Revival, Lady Huntingdon was able to dedicate a greater part of her time to caring for her students. Her aging body did not deter her—letter after letter she wrote to them as she received news of their disappointments and triumphs in the field. Right before Trevecca had opened, another ambitious project that was to consume her energy and time, the Countess had confided to Whitefield:

> Very low and ill I have been since I came to this place or should have wrote to you. Such I continue, but an old servant does not cease doing his master's work because he is not so well able to perform it, but continues to work on till he can work no longer ... I would fain do and though perhaps only to lay the foundations. Others He may appoint to build

---

[27] Cook, *Countess of Huntingdon*, 303
[28] Cook, *Countess of Huntingdon*, 303-304.

The Bold Evangelist

thereon and He will have my voice and heart in saying and feeling. He cannot have a poorer or more helpless a creature for His services, and yet I do say to Him I will do it as well as ever I can.[29]

The foundation that the Countess had laid led many passing through her college to continue on as fruitful ministers, be it in her chapels, parish churches, or Dissenting meeting houses. Her foundation would also lead to the development of other colleges like it and was yet another means of infusing spiritual vitality into the religious life of eighteenth-century England.

---

[29] Tyson, *Lady Huntingdon and Her Correspondence*, 109.

12
The Minutes Controversy

John Berridge, sensitive to the reality of spiritual warfare waging all around, had advised Selina about the need to be prepared for trials. Months after her college's grand opening, Berridge, who could always be relied on for his candor, wrote a letter of caution:

> You may therefore rejoice, but rejoice with trembling. Faithful laborers may be expected from thence ... but I believe the sensible comfort will not last always, nor long; neither is it convenient. In the present state of things, a winter is as much wanted to continue the earth fruitful as summer. If the grass was always growing, it would soon grow to nothing; just as flowers, that blow much and long, generally blow themselves to death. And as it is thus with the ground, so it is with the labourers too. Afflictions, desertions, and temptations are as needful as consolations... Jesus has given you a hand and a heart to execute great things for His glory, and therefore He will deal you out a suitable measure of afflictions to keep your balance steady.[1]

Devastating events came to pass that proved the weight of Berridge's words. The Minutes Controversy, which erupted two years after the inauguration of Trevecca, caused a big split in the Evangelical Revival. It started in August 1770 when John Wesley held his twenty-seventh Annual Conference in London. The focus of the meeting was on the divergences in doctrine between members of the Revival.

---

[1] Tyson, *Lady Huntingdon and Her Correspondence*, 159.

The Bold Evangelist

The Document that Started the Controversy

The stirring accounts of the conversions of George Whitefield, the Wesleys, and Benjamin Ingham pictured their humble embrace of God's free grace. As they had learned back in their days in the Holy Club, any attempt to do good works to earn the favor of God was futile. Salvation was on the basis of God's grace alone—in theological terms, the sinner was justified by faith. But the issues raised at the London conference brought into question John Wesley's position on this fundamental truth. The tragedy in the controversy was that much of it was a result of misunderstanding and failure to practice restraint when the conflict first broke out. Wesley had published the *Minutes* after the conference and when it was read by members of the Revival, many were disturbed by its contents—even close associates of Wesley were uncomfortable with it. The problem lay in the ambiguity of his words regarding the nature of salvation and the role of good works in the life of the believer. Excerpts from Wesley's *Minutes* reveal why it was such a cause of concern:

> We have received it as a maxim that "a man is to do nothing in order to justification." Nothing can be more false. Whoever desires to find favour with God should "cease from evil and learn to do well." Whoever repents should do "works meet for repentance." And if this is not in order to find favour, what does he do them for? ...
>
> Who of us is **now** accepted of God?
> He that now believes in Christ with a loving and obedient heart. ...
>
> Is not this salvation by works?
> Not by the **merit** of works, but by works as a **condition**. ...
>
> But how are we sure, that the person in question never did fear God or work righteousness?

The Minutes Controversy

His own saying so is not proof; for we know, how all that are convinced of sin undervalue themselves in every respect.

Does not talking of a justified or a sanctified **state** tend to mislead men? Almost naturally leading them to trust in what was done in one moment?
Whereas we are every hour and every moment pleasing or displeasing to God, "according to our works"; according to the whole of our inward tempers, and our outward behaviour.[2]

The Countess outrightly opposed the *Minutes*, it appearing to convey that works played a part in salvation, which ran contrary to the basic conviction of the Methodist movement (or for that matter the Protestant Reformation). Without asking for further explanation of Wesley's intended meaning behind the *Minutes* and validating whether this was indeed what he had meant, Lady Huntingdon automatically assumed that Wesley's statements were heretical and demanded that he retract them. At this point a gracious act on the part of either side might have alleviated the situation. But it was only going to get worse before it got better. Wesley was no longer welcomed to preach in any of the Countess' chapels, nor was he invited to the second anniversary of Trevecca College to take place only weeks after the publication of the *Minutes*.[3]

Rather than clarifying the matter with the Countess and assuring her that he was by no means elevating works over faith, Wesley had acted with equal callousness. His was in the form of a letter that expressed his frank evaluation of her and her labors. The letter, however, no longer exists: the Countess was so offended by it that she disposed of it soon after.[4] Based on the reaction of her friends and Wesley's own reference to it in his letter to Joseph

---

[2] Cook, *Countess of Huntingdon*, 278–279.
[3] Cook, *Countess of Huntingdon*, 280.
[4] Cook, *Countess of Huntingdon*, 275.

Benson months after, we know that Wesley wrote of his disapproval of the Countess' alleged pride as well as other observed weaknesses.[5] John Fletcher, Howell Harris, Walter Shirley[6]—and even Charles Wesley—were all shocked by John's harsh tone. Yet John, even when enough time had passed for him to assess his own actions, was convinced that he had not erred in sending the letter, holding that he was only speaking the truth in love and that his directness in reproving the Countess was *his* Christian duty and for *her* gain.

Overtones of the *Minutes* Document

While the published *Minutes* had sparked the dispute, there were other explanations for why the controversy had escalated to the extent that it did. The representatives, John and Selina, were both strong-headed individuals, and even early in their friendship, a distance between them was detected. Another explanation is that the Countess' status and financial resources made Trevecca College possible, and already noted is that John likely resented her for being able to realize a plan that he had wanted to undertake for himself.[7]

Selina and John were also on different sides of the Methodist movement. Although the Calvinist-Arminian distinction was not in the foreground of the *Minutes* document, it was no doubt a driving force in its creation. The role of works in salvation was understood differently depending on which side one stood. For the Calvinist, no measure of works leads to salvation, but it is by the sovereign act of God given to the undeserving sinner. For the Arminian, the former part is also true, but human freewill works in conjunction with God's sovereignty to bring about salvation. While

---

[5] Wesley, *Letters*, 5:215, quoted in Cook, *Countess of Huntingdon*, 276–277.

[6] Walter Shirley was Lady Huntingdon's cousin and would become her chaplain following George Whitefield's death.

[7] Cook, *Countess of Huntingdon*, 274.

The Minutes Controversy

both held dear the justification by faith doctrine—from the Calvinist's standpoint, God chose the individual for salvation; from the Arminian's standpoint, the individual chose.

The Real Meaning behind the *Minutes*

This doctrinal difference had already been seen in the dispute that took place decades earlier between John Wesley and George Whitefield. Wesley's aim in circulating the *Minutes* can be better understood in light of what was at issue then. Wesley, in actuality, was not so much advocating that salvation was in some way dependent on good works, but rather was focusing on the importance of working out the Christian faith by way of good works.

"Who of us is now accepted of God? He that now believes in Christ with a loving and obedient heart ... His own saying so is not proof." That is to say, a loving and obedient heart is what proves that the faith of the believer is genuine, for it reflects the believer's faith in Christ and life in the Spirit. A mere profession of faith is not enough in the sense that it risks being shallow. Wesley's fear had always been that if Calvinism widened its reach, so would the faith community's negligence of the pursuit of holiness. If it was God who chose and not the individual, he believed that the false assurance of salvation would inevitably lead to spiritual slackness, or in theological terms, antinomianism.

Sad Consequences of the Controversy

Eventually the issue was brought back to Trevecca, but by this time the controversy had changed its course—it became a confrontation between Calvinists and Arminians. It must be emphasized again that the Countess' initial objective was to establish an institution for ministry training to serve the Methodist movement as a whole. Fletcher upheld Arminian convictions, and so did the resident tutor she appointed in 1770, Joseph Benson (1749–1821). But when the controversy broke out, the Countess required that those at the college state where they stood with Wesley's *Minutes*. Since Benson acknowledged he saw no fault in the document, he was dismissed in 1771, as was a portion of the student body that was of Arminian conviction. This dismissal was followed by an even greater loss—Fletcher's own resignation: "If 'every Arminian must quit the college,' I am actually discharged also."[8]

Of John Wesley's *Minutes* Fletcher admitted that there was a lack of discretion in the choice of words, but the principles laid out were in no way contrary to Scripture. His letter to the Countess in March 1771 confirms that it was out of concern with the dangers of antinomianism that the *Minutes* was necessary, and even further, for preventing it from seeping into the college:

> I cannot disavow the doctrines [Mr. Wesley's Minutes] fairly contain, any more than I dare reject some parts of St. James's Epistles ... the extract of the Minutes is so excessively short, the subject is so exceedingly delicate, and some of the expressions so unguarded, that at first sight it carries a strong appearance of legality, as at such I do disapprove of it; but far from thinking it incompatible with salvation by faith, upon close examination, I do not find in it one proposition more apparently suited to the Pharisaical taste, than those which are contained in Jam II.21,22, 24, Act. X.35, Rev.II:5, 10, John 1.9 ... And many such places, where the Antinomian error is guarded against.[9]

Fletcher's conscience did not permit him to stay, but his letter shows that he nonetheless hoped for peace between the parties:

> I still declare Mr. Wesley shall be welcome to my pulpit, and I shall think myself honoured in giving him and every Gospel minister (whether an Arminian or a Calvinist) the right hand of fellowship. As Lady Huntingdon declared to me last

---

[8] Cook, *Countess of Huntingdon*, 287.
[9] Tyson, *Lady Huntingdon and Her Correspondence*, 169.

The Minutes Controversy

night, with the highest degree of positiveness, that whosoever did not fully and absolutely disavow and renounce the doctrine contained in Mr. Wesley's Minutes, should not upon any terms, stay in her college ... I should not act the part of an honest man if I did not absolutely resign my charge, and take my leave of this seminary of persons learning which I do with a heart full of ardent wishes ... I sincerely remain in the bond of the gospel of peace, and trust shall always remain, Her Ladyship's dutiful the most though unprofitable and unworthy servant.[10]

Fletcher's departure was a terrible blow to Trevecca. The college was to lose an exemplary servant and leader of the Church, and Lady Huntingdon was never able to find a suitable candidate to replace him. Even under such unfortunate circumstances, the graciousness of Fletcher still shone, for he could say of the Countess' misguided actions: "I look upon Lady Huntingdon as an eminent servant of God, an honest, gracious person, but not above the reach of prejudice; and where prejudice misleads her, her warm heart makes her go rather too fast," and in a letter consoling Benson following his dismissal, "Remember that great lady has been an instrument of great good, and that there are great inconsistencies attending the greatest and best of men."[11]

Further Offences and Miscalculated Actions

The controversy did not begin to simmer until after the Countess and Walter Shirley decided to protest against the *Minutes* at Wesley's next conference. A letter circulated in the public soliciting anyone who sided with them to join the protest. The decision was gravely imprudent, which could be seen by Charles Wesley's response upon receiving the letter, as he marked on it, "Lady Huntingdon's LAST," thereby discontinuing any further

---

[10] Tyson, *Lady Huntingdon and Her Correspondence*, 169.
[11] Cook, *Countess of Huntingdon*, 288.

correspondence with his long-time friend.[12] The rally against his brother was a step too far. As the day of Wesley's conference drew closer, however, the Countess finally realized her miscalculated steps and both she and Shirley apologized to John Wesley for it (she and Charles reunited a few years later). Instead of a protest, Shirley along with others attended the conference to discuss the issue. The meeting ended peaceably. Shirley publicly apologized for the misinterpretation of the *Minutes* while John Wesley, with over 50 other preachers, signed a declaration affirming the justification by faith doctrine.[13]

Meanwhile Fletcher was unaware that the controversy had reached a diplomatic conclusion—at least not until it was too late. Witness to the unreasonable reaction to Wesley and grieved by the events that unraveled at Trevecca, Fletcher wrote a strong defense of Wesley and the *Minutes*, which Wesley then decided to publish. Not until then did Fletcher learn of the signed declaration and immediately tried to put a stop to the printing of his text (entitled *Vindication of the Minutes of 1770*); he even attempted to absorb the printing costs but to no avail.[14] In writing the defense, Fletcher had desired, above all, for both sides to reconcile.

The aftereffects of the controversy lingered for years, with some of the involved parties exchanging spiteful words.[15] The Countess kept out of the conflict, at one point expressing her displeasure with the indiscreet exchanges. Trevecca's stance was also altered, from then on only accepting those holding to Calvinistic convictions, which impacted its capacity to reach a wider circle within the Methodist movement. The two sides went their separate ways in their ministries.

---

[12] Cook, *Countess of Huntingdon*, 291.
[13] Cook, *Countess of Huntingdon*, 294.
[14] Cook, *Countess of Huntingdon*, 295.
[15] Cook, *Countess of Huntingdon*, 297.

The Minutes Controversy

Poetic Words of Wisdom from John Fletcher

Embarking on the year that Trevecca was to open, Fletcher had written to Lady Huntingdon about all that was before them and affirmed that whatever was to unravel was within the sovereign care of God, which meant they could march into the uncertain future with resolute trust:

> What this year may bring forth who knows? This, however, we know—all will be welcome that he shall be pleased to appoint; and nothing will befall us but by his appointment, for the very hairs of our head are numbered. With what angelic peace and martyr-like intrepidity ought this consideration to inspire us! Oh, for more faith to persevere.
>
> Oh, pray for me, insensible me, that the Holy Ghost may teach me to sound the depths of incarnate love, or at least to lose myself in their immensity, together with your Ladyship. It is an ocean without bottom: may we fall into it every moment, as insignificant drops of gall, to be absorbed in those pure and mighty waters. There the mountains of our iniquities and the valleys of our deficiencies are more effectually covered than the highest mountains were by the waters of the flood. Our temptations, transgression, losses, and pains are lost here like drops or showers in the sea. We are in this sea: it fills heaven and earth; and if we meet now and then in it with a dash against the rock of adversity, or a storm from the boisterous winds of temptations, it is only to make our scum go from us, as Isaiah says. Welcome, then, even contrary winds; they are, in reality, favourable. Some will, no doubt, blow upon your Ladyship from that little point of the compass, Trevecca; but the Lord hath them in His hands; fear not, the government is still upon His shoulder.[16]

Fletcher may not have foreseen the upsetting events that were to befall Trevecca, yet he knew of the realities of living in a fallen

---

[16] Tyson, *Lady Huntingdon and Her Correspondence*, 161.

The Bold Evangelist

world. The unsightly flaws and foul errors of redeemed sinners—Fletcher reminded his dear friend—are but mere drops in the ocean of God's mercy and grace, for in these pure and mighty waters are they cleansed by the blood of Jesus Christ their Saviour.

13
The Bethesda Orphan House

The Death of George Whitefield

As the Minutes Controversy was about to begin in August 1770, the life of George Whitefield was to near its end. The great preacher died on the thirtieth of September. It was not until more than a month later that the Countess, who was at Trevecca College at the time, discovered the news in the papers before anyone could personally inform her. So anguished was she by the news of her good friend's death, she at once sought the consolation of Howell Harris at the college. She was weeping and beseeched him to speak with her on the subject, which Harris was hesitant to do, himself equally distraught; but as a fellow Christian brother he gathered himself and did as she asked.[1]

It was Whitefield's wish for his friend John Wesley to perform the funeral service in England, his final gesture of peace. Charles Wesley penned an elegy to pay tribute to this servant of God, expressing the sorrow and esteem of the countless upon whose lives he touched.

Whitefield's Orphanage in Georgia

Whitefield's absence must have been gravely felt by Selina during the course of the Minutes Controversy; his irenic nature and godly counsel might have been the precise guidance she needed to face the confrontations between her and John Wesley. But this was not to be so. He had sailed to America in 1769 and was not in England when the conflict arose. While he was actively preaching, his health had been declining; toward the end of his life, friends and spectators alike would express their concern about whether

---

[1] Welch, *Spiritual Pilgrim*, 131.

The Bold Evangelist

he was well enough to continue. But in Whitefield fashion, he pressed on. One of his biggest projects—the Bethesda Orphan House—was a testament to his endurance and dedication. His aspiration to set up an orphanage dated back to 1737 during John and Charles Wesley's first missionary trip to Georgia when Charles witnessed the area rife with sickness and death. Many children were left abandoned and helpless after losing their parents. Charles wrote a letter to Whitefield in England about the colony's desperate conditions and this planted a seed in the minister's heart to be a defender of their cause[2] (*Bethesda* means "House of Mercy").

Whitefield had taken the proposal of the Georgian trustees for the establishment of the orphanage to England and was granted permission to raise the necessary funds. Travelling through England, Scotland and Wales for his preaching tours, he presented the vision and solicited financial support (the Countess of Huntingdon was among Bethesda's early supporters).[3] Whitefield was optimistic. By 1740 he had enough to set the project in motion and construction began in March. Over forty orphans were to be housed in Bethesda upon its opening.[4] The orphanage was built 10 miles north of Savannah, Georgia and occupied 500 acres of land. The structures themselves consisted of a main building that was two stories high with 20 spacious rooms, and two smaller buildings, one an infirmary and the other a workhouse.

As far as its day-to-day activities, Bethesda thrived: the children were schooled in Latin, arithmetic, writing and reading and were expected to adhere to a strict schedule of when to rise, wash, have their meals, and tend to their chores. Their spiritual

---

[2] Edward J. Cashin, *Beloved Bethesda: A History of George Whitefield's Home for Boys, 1740-2000* (Georgia: Mercer University, 2001), 3.

[3] Cook, *Countess of Huntingdon*, 317.

[4] J. Gillies, *Memoirs of the Life of the Rev. George Whitefield* (London: 1772), 50, 51, quoted in Welch, *Spiritual Pilgrim*.

The Bethesda Orphan House

wellbeing was of prime importance as they were expected to participate in public prayer, hymn-singing, and scripture reading. Financially sustaining the operation of Bethesda, however, was more complicated. Whitefield depended heavily on donations and much of this came from Dissenters in Georgia, who represented the majority of the religious population. In addition to receiving academic instruction, the orphans were trained in cotton-picking and spinning to secure further income. The most controversial issue by far was Whitefield's belief that the establishment could only be feasibly sustained by the use of slaves. Slavery was illegal when the new Georgia colony was first founded, but Whitefield, along with others, petitioned for the law to be lifted, maintaining that the colony's success depended on such affordable labor (the law was reversed in 1750).[5] But even amid all these efforts, Bethesda accumulated massive debts.

Lady Huntingdon Inherits Bethesda

The future state of the orphanage, and Whitefield's further plans of erecting a public educational institution alongside it, was still not settled at the time of his death. But Whitefield passed on his hopes of realizing his vision to his trusted friend Selina Hastings—his high esteem of her character evident not only by the statement in his will but in the very act of handing off his beloved project to her.

> In respect to my outward American concerns which I have engaged in simply and solely for His great name sake, I leave that Building commonly called the Orphan-House at Bethesda in the Province of Georgia together with all the other buildings lately erected thereon… to that Elect Lady, that Mother in Israel, that Mirror of true and undefiled religion the right Honourable Selina Countess Dowager of

---

[5] Harding, *Selina, Countess of Huntingdon*, 148.

> Huntingdon; desiring that as soon as may be after my decease the plan of the intended Orphan-House Bethesda College may be prosecuted, or, if not practicable or eligible, to pursue the present plan of the Orphan-House Academy on its Old Foundation, and the usual channel.[6]

In addition to the Bethesda property, the Countess inherited "all other buildings, lands, Negroes, books, [and] furniture." Fifty slaves came into her possession, and up until her death those numbers rose.[7] Britain was an active participant in the slave trade in the eighteenth-century and its horrors were gradually being recognized by prominent figures in the Evangelical world. John Wesley was an influential spokesperson against the practice, publishing an article entitled *Thoughts on Slavery* in 1774, in which he vehemently charged the guilty of their inhumanity: "Are you *a man*? Then you should have a *human* heart … When you saw the flowing eyes, the heaving breasts, the bleeding sides and tortured limbs of your fellow-creatures, were you a stone, or a brute?" Whitefield, although a partaker in the modification of the slavery law in Georgia, was nonetheless outraged by his witness of the mistreatment of slaves on the plantations and opposed the abuse by way of a letter addressed to the inhabitants of the American colonies. Its content was later published in their newspapers:

> Is it not the highest ingratitude as well as cruelty, not to let your poor slaves enjoy some fruits of their labour? Whilst I have viewed your plantations cleared and cultivated, and have seen many spacious houses, and the owners of them faring sumptuously every day, my blood has almost run cold within me, when I have considered how many of your slaves have neither convenient food to eat, nor proper raiment to

---

[6] Tyson, *Lady Huntingdon and Her Correspondence*, 214.
[7] Harding, *Selina, Countess of Huntingdon*, 148.

The Bethesda Orphan House

put on, notwithstanding most of the comforts you enjoy were solely owing to their indefatigable labours.[8]

In light of the charitable acts that were evident in the lives of Whitefield and Lady Huntingdon, explanation is needed for their acceptance of slaves to support their philanthropic and evangelistic ends. Dependence on slave labor was prevalent and deeply entrenched in the economics of society: arriving to the conviction that the practice needed to be abolished often came from a rude awakening—as witnessed in the compelling accounts of evangelicals William Wilberforce (1759-1833) and former slave ship captain John Newton (1725-1807), men who became leaders in the campaign against slavery. Newton explained how it was possible that he could have remained ignorant and participated in such a practice:

> Disagreeable I had long found it; but I think I should have quitted it sooner, had I considered it, as I now do, to be unlawful and wrong. But I never had a scruple upon this head, at the time; nor was such a thought once suggested to me, by any friend. What I did, I did ignorantly; considering it as the line of life which Divine Providence had allotted to me, and having no concern, in point of conscience, but to treat the Slaves, while under my care, with as much humanity, as a regard to my own safety would admit ... The Slave Trade was always unjustifiable; but inattention and interest prevented, for a time, the evil from being perceived.[9]

For Whitefield and Lady Huntingdon, the abuse suffered by the slaves appalled them, but rather than going against the system itself, they believed that they could reform the system from within. Releasing the slaves would return them to similarly impoverished

---

[8] Dallimore, *George Whitefield*, 79.

[9] John Coffey, "Evangelicals, Slavery & the Slave Trade: From Whitefield to Wilberforce," *ANVIL* 24.2 (2007): 97–116.

conditions, and, subjected to the irreligion of the world, the prospect of exposing them to Christianity would be lost. Better, they supposed, to keep the slaves under their care and within their sphere of influence.[10] Blinded they were to the cruelty of those in the community who did not share their views and whose slaves as a result bore unspeakable torment.[11]

The Countess' New Mission

Left to the Countess was also the financially bleak situation of Bethesda: it was thousands of pounds in debt when it came into her hands. The discouraging state of affairs, however, was not a deterrent; she had the option of passing up on the property but instead was keen on achieving its potential. Having always been committed to seeing to the spread of the gospel, she began to formulate her own vision for the property. Just before her friend's death, a bill was in the process of being passed to allow for Whitefield's plans for his college, but the Countess, upon consulting with others, determined not to resume the bill. Her desire was to bring the good news to the settlers and Indians of Georgia.[12] She wanted to establish a college that would provide ministerial training to produce a ready supply of missionaries to work the field in America. The Countess' eagerness to plunge into such an enterprise likely stemmed from her experience in founding Trevecca: the fruit born by her college in Wales granted her the confidence and ambition to replicate the mission elsewhere.[13]

But noble as the enterprise was, the Countess failed to fully consider the barriers that stood between the viability of

---

[10] Welch, *Spiritual Pilgrim*, 145.

[11] During a time when colonists were unwilling to publish poetry by an African-American, the poet Phillis Wheatley (1753-1784) when in England turned to Lady Huntingdon, who became a patroness of Wheatley's book *Poems on Various Subjects, Religious and Moral* (1773). Wheatley dedicated the book to the Countess.

[12] Welch, *Spiritual Pilgrim*, 134-135.

[13] Harding, *Selina, Countess of Huntingdon*, 149.

The Bethesda Orphan House

establishing a foreign mission base and the realities of executing such a project from across the Atlantic. Her letter to Charles Eccles, one of the clergymen she had sent to work in Bethesda, did indicate that she was not entirely unaware of the limitations of the mission: "The great distance of Wales adds to those difficulties, as you cannot be assured of the exactness of those you entrust."[14] But neither she nor any of the others involved would have foreseen the magnitude of the problems that would come to pass. The Countess herself was ultimately never able to visit America, though her letters show how much she wanted to. She was 63-years-old when the Bethesda property was bequeathed to her, and while she expressed her wish to board a ship herself and address the unfavorable reports she received from her team in America, she was advised against it, her ill health not possibly being able to endure the grueling journey. How restless and fretful Selina must have felt at times to be in a state of uncertainty about a treasured mission over which she had little control: "O! that His glory or some display of it might appear. Suspense is the painfulest situation on earth. In all Love the Lord shall appear to His poor blind, waiting servants."[15]

Obstacles and Setbacks of the Mission

The Countess never imagined that the leader she assigned to the mission—William Piercy—one of her own clergymen, would be among the source of her problems. Her letter in November 1772 to William Tennent III (1740-1777), a pastor of a church in Charleston, South Carolina and a member of the Provincial Congress, expressed her esteem of Piercy's character:

> I have by this ventured to introduce Mr. Piercy, who I have made President of the College in Georgia, believing from his

---

[14] Tyson, *Lady Huntingdon and Her Correspondence*, 215.
[15] Tyson, *Lady Huntingdon and Her Correspondence*, 218.

The Bold Evangelist

great abilities, his most blessed disinterested zeal for the cause of Christ, and the great and eminent preacher he is of the glorious Gospel of Christ, he will be most acceptable to all who love the Lord Jesus Christ in sincerity.[16]

Even the seven individuals from Trevecca who came forward to commit themselves to the mission placed their trust in Piercy. The representatives who made it to Georgia included John Cosson (who was to be superintendent of the estate), Joseph Cook, Daniel Roberts, William White, Lewis Richards, Thomas Hill, and Betty Hughes (the housekeeper)—all of them were young, Piercy himself not even thirty.[17] But they were ready to make the sacrifice, a decision that meant leaving behind all that was familiar and embarking upon the unknown, which upon their arrival would end up mightily shaking their hopes. The events that took place prior to their departure, however, had painted a picture that all that lay ahead was to be promising. An extended ceremony, filled with prayer, hymn-singing, preaching, and celebration, was held to commit the mission to the Lord, this on top of further commissioning at Whitefield's Tottenham Court Road Chapel and an elaborate sendoff for the party which was scheduled to set sail on 27 October 1772.

Complications striking just before the journey—sickness, unfavourable weather conditions that led to delays, and confusion of personal schedules—wound up fragmenting the party into three groups so that they travelled to Georgia separately: the first comprised Joseph Cook, John Cosson, and Betty Hughes; the second, the remaining students from Trevecca; and the third, William Piercy, his brother Richard Piercy, Charles Eccles (who was to be schoolmaster of the college) and his wife. The first group arrived in the Savannah river in December 1772 and the second shortly

---

[16] Tyson, *Lady Huntingdon and Her Correspondence*, 215.
[17] Cook, *Countess of Huntingdon*, 319-320.

The Bethesda Orphan House

after, with Piercy's not arriving until months later in March. John Cosson's group was the first to witness the devastating conditions of Bethesda: the rooms lacked furniture and sheets to accommodate them and the estate was short of livestock to provide them nourishing food. With resources scarce, the group warned the other students to stay in England.[18] Responding to Cosson's report of the bleak conditions, Lady Huntingdon expressed her distress and concern, but encouraged him to rely on divine strength to persevere in the mission:

> Nothing can be more disturbing than your account given of Georgia College ... But when I think of all your trials of this faith and also that patience you must be endued with before the promises can be accomplished, I tenderly feel for all, and indeed at times as much as you all unitedly can do. I can't say an hour in the day passes without some prayer, some wish or some distressing fear or cheerful hope by intervals possess me for you, and the distance so great that months must pass without hearing that I look upon my situation as difficult to bear as yours can be. However, may the Lord enable as us all, that in all and through all we may be found faithful to what He has called us to and then in His will and way we shall have cause living or dying to glorify Him through the great tribulation He has appointed for us.[19]

Cosson's group used the opportunity to preach to the slaves on the plantation. When Piercy and his group arrived, Piercy was disappointed by the Bethesda property, though he did not consider its conditions as awful as the others did. Inexperienced and accustomed to the comparatively luxurious lodgings at Trevecca, the students were shocked by their meager and strange surroundings,

---

[18] Cook, *Countess of Huntingdon*, 322.
[19] Tyson, *Lady Huntingdon and Her Correspondence*, 218–219.

some lamenting over their decision and aching to return to England.

The desperate situation was exacerbated by the fact that Piercy became dictatorial in his treatment of the students, who cried out to the Countess about their leader's behavior. Desiring to make the most of their situation, they hoped to enter into the back settlements to minister to the Indians, but Piercy forbade them to go. In circumstances where students most needed guidance and support, they instead received disparagement, their spiritual readiness questioned by their own leader. Travelling along the Georgian coast preaching in local churches and gaining a positive reception, Piercy had developed a puffed up view of himself, reckoning that he was to become the next George Whitefield.[20]

The Countess' Heartfelt Appeal to Piercy

Lady Huntingdon was profoundly troubled by the accounts of Piercy's conduct and her letter to him in September 1773, less than a year since the mission in Georgia began, demonstrates that her love for her students was truly like that of a mother for her children. Her maternal instinct was to protect them. She was deeply conflicted by the situation, hearing contradicting reports from both sides yet being too far away to offer a swift (or any) resolution. At this point she still gave Piercy the benefit of the doubt and directed him to the One whom all Christian servants must give account. The pain washing her words reflects her devotion to the students:

> The distance is so great that I can be no judge of events that can be satisfactory to you, while I should rejoice to do was it in my power as to the difficulties relative to the students. This is weighty indeed. They are far from happy, and unless a spirit of love and tenderness rests over them they will find

---

[20] Cook, *Countess of Huntingdon*, 324.

The Bethesda Orphan House

their way back to me. They complain of bondage and are not at sufficient liberty. I do think to venture for the Lord and am so uneasy that I am distressed above all things to know what to do.

They have been used by me so kindly that they will not bear an unnecessary severity ... This trial for me exceeds all others as I know not how to act with the feelings of my love for them and that by so doing I should appear to disapprove anything you do. O! My dear friend, the Lord will have a free and hospitable spirit. The letters of these late packets distress me more than ever I was yet, as I find they only stay upon my account and are greatly disquieted by that state of servitude they seem to groan under ...

I find by their letters and though there is much reason of reproof for those things you mention, love and entreaties I do believe would in time come over them, but anything upon the foot of great authority will in the end cause them all to leave you. And my distress is so great to support your authority and at the same time not cast them off, must be a cruel way for me to walk in, knowing what they have suffered cheerfully and willing with you in this work for me.

O! My dear friend, we must be servants of all. This must be our spirit before the Lord, willingly for His sake suffer what we will from it. The proud He does and will resist but giveth grace to the humble. I know you will forgive as I can know nothing but by theirs and your representations, and I wish for only that light which might approve that which is most excellent ... Be patient towards all men and making the best of all things we can knowing we are with all our infirmity yet in the body; indeed my spirits are so low and so depressed that I do suffer inexpressibly, expecting every ship may bring them back and not knowing what to do and lest you should take anything unkind, as you do know that must hurt me in the most tender manner to do this.[21]

---

[21] Tyson, *Lady Huntingdon and Her Correspondence*, 224.

Compassion Guides a Student to the Cross

The harshness of Piercy and the kindheartedness of the Countess were also apparent following a shocking event that took place not long after the team arrived in Georgia. Upon their arrival John Cosson and Betty Hughes had requested James Habersham (who had been Whitefield's co-laborer in Georgia) to marry them. Rumors had already been circulating that Betty was with child and they were confirmed when a mere four months after the marriage ceremony the couple gave birth to a baby boy. Although Cosson explained to Piercy that he and Betty had married in secret at Trevecca the year before, Piercy refused to accept his explanation and was so incensed that he banished the couple from the premises, leaving the new mother with no shelter to care for her child. Cosson was dismissed and was to go back to England to offer his account to the Countess.

Discovering that Cosson was truly remorseful, Lady Huntingdon pardoned him for his conduct. He had confided to her about how the shame and humiliation were crushing him. The graciousness extended to him by the Countess ushered him into the forgiving embrace of the Heavenly Father.[22] Cosson, repentant over his actions, felt the freeing power of the gospel. What helped restore him was Lady Huntingdon's love and her understanding of the real battle of sin in the believer's life. Cosson was to return to Bethesda, both his return fare to England and back to Georgia assumed by the Countess. Betty expressed her thanks in a letter.

Sadly the Countess' pardon of the Cossons did nothing to abate Piercy's ill will toward the couple. Although Cosson was hoping to resume his ministry in Georgia, Piercy made sure that this would not happen, publicly denouncing him, ultimately rendering Cosson's labor ineffectual.[23] Within two years since the

---

[22] Cook, *Countess of Huntingdon*, 324.
[23] Cook, *Countess of Huntingdon*, 324.

The Bethesda Orphan House

students' arrival, all of them left Bethesda or moved on to minister elsewhere among the local Dissenters.

Resistance of Local Dissenters to the Countess' Mission

The students were not the only victims of Piercy's autocracy. Piercy was accountable for escalating the already embittered relations between the Countess' team and local Dissenters.[24] When deciding to set up her college in Georgia, the Countess did not take into account how her enterprise appeared to the residents. While Whitefield had been in America, he had established close relations with the Dissenters there, which was why they were Bethesda's main benefactors.[25] Denominational differences did not prevent the Anglican clergyman from forming bonds with others so long as the individuals or groups revealed themselves to be genuine followers of Christ. When plans were being made to establish the Countess' college for the training of ministers, its President to be one of *her* clergymen, the locals interpreted the venture as an attempt to widen the rule of the Anglican Church. In fact, even Whitefield did not succeed in securing a royal charter in England for his college because the Archbishop required that an Anglican be appointed as head, a stipulation that was not acceptable to the Georgian colony given its religious constituents.[26] A letter written in 1773 to the Countess from William Tennent III uncovers the dissatisfaction of the Dissenters with her actions:

> The dissenters have been herewith steady friends of Mr. Whitefield, as we conceive that he had the interest of souls at heart and as the Lord evidenceth, owned his labours. We have obtained no small respect for you, Madam, as one of the very few nobles who zealously support the truth ... how far this part of your Ladyship's plan is calculated to promote

---

[24] Harding, *Selina, Countess of Huntingdon*, 153.
[25] Cook, *Countess of Huntingdon*, 324.
[26] Tyson, *Lady Huntingdon and Her Correspondence*, 212.

religion in this country you may judge from the following facts: ...at least two thirds of the inhabitants are Dissenters ... That which opens a door in England and Wales to the Methodists only obstructs it here ... Is it not really unjust that those estates which were given mostly by the Dissenters should be improved entirely to the purposes of Conformity and that with no other reason than that your Ladyship happens to be of the Religion established in England?[27]

So on the evening of 30 May 1773 when a fire broke out at Bethesda that brought most of the estate to ruins, many who were already losing hope in or opposing the mission saw the incident as a sign. Tennent, for example, concluded in the same letter,

> Would it not seem from these considerations that Providence now [given the fire] gave the fairest opening to remove at once the offence and to place the intended College in a more favourable situation. Perhaps the only reason that should entice you to fix your College there is now removed.[28]

Habersham reported the news to the Countess—books in the library, a wax statue of Whitefield, house and chapel furniture, and communion items—all were burnt, and if not, plundered. Fortunately only a handful of people were on site when the fire broke out and no one was fatally hurt. Arson was suspected, though with no proof speculation was pointless. Habersham was one of the few who remained optimistic about the event:

> I am very hopeful, that the great Head of the Church will appear for this institution, and that the many prayers and tears offered up on its behalf will not be lost, and that, if I

---

[27] Tyson, *Lady Huntingdon and Her Correspondence*, 221.
[28] Tyson, *Lady Huntingdon and Her Correspondence*, 222.

The Bethesda Orphan House

may be allowed the expression, the second Temple will be restored with greater lustre than the first.[29]

Habersham, who had served alongside Whitefield since almost the beginning of his ministry in America, longed to fulfill his dear friend's lifelong vision.

The Situation Escalates with the Outbreak of War

The Countess was disheartened—she had already invested a substantial amount in Bethesda. The fire was a serious setback and reconstruction would be costly. Presenting a positive outlook on the situation, Piercy urged the Countess to rebuild, detailing missionary opportunities and financially viable options for the estate.[30] Rebuild the Countess did. She was still not fully aware of Piercy's self-serving schemes. Bethesda continued to operate ably until the War of American Independence arose in 1775 when American colonies fought to separate themselves from Britain—the British government's highhanded taxation of the colonies led to their resistance. In 1778 Georgia was apprehended, along with the Bethesda estate; so between the years 1775 and 1777, all correspondence between the Countess and her Georgian contacts ceased.[31] The Georgian colony remained occupied by the British until 1782, and had it not been for the Countess' support of the colonists, her estate would also have been seized.[32]

Seeking refuge amid the violence in nearby South Carolina, Piercy had abandoned Bethesda in 1779. He eventually made his way back to England, and soon his deceitful activities came to light. At first he attempted to win back the Countess' favor, defending his actions in Georgia, drawing attention to his efforts in

---

[29] Tyson, *Lady Huntingdon and Her Correspondence*, 220.
[30] Cook, *Countess of Huntingdon*, 327.
[31] Harding, *Selina, Countess of Huntingdon*, 157.
[32] Welch, *Spiritual Pilgrim*, 147.

caring for the estate. But when evaluating his financial accounts as well as reports from others who were witness to his fraudulent actions in America (including his own brother Richard)[33], Lady Huntingdon went from doubting him to defending herself from him. During his time away, Piercy had never informed the Countess of his expenses, but now he was demanding that he be compensated for his work all those years in America. Lady Huntingdon expressed to a friend in Georgia her disbelief upon discovering Piercy's true colors:

> Art, guile and the most shameless fraud joined with the most unceasing untruths has but the sad evidences of a character for ten years past of the most uncommon instances of unfaithfulness and bad practices that ever the most simple and Christian confidence has met with.[34]

Her heart was most broken when she imagined that the money Piercy had pocketed for himself was bread meant for her "poor, dear orphans' mouths," and further, a "sad abuse" of her "old and dear friend's trust" to her. Yet her defense for not acting sooner was that she was much too far away to assess fairly the claims made against Piercy and Piercy's own descriptions: "my total ignorance of these matters left a reasonable claim upon me to wait for proofs that could best satisfy me in the justice of my own conduct."

The Outcome of the Mission
When all accounts were laid bare upon Piercy's return, the Countess was prepared to act. In June 1783 Piercy proposed that the dispute go to arbitration, which she agreed to:

---

[33] Welch, *Spiritual Pilgrim*, 166.
[34] Tyson, *Lady Huntingdon and Her Correspondence*, 237, May 13, 1784.

The Bethesda Orphan House

"If I have wronged any man I am willing to restore him fourfold" [Luke 19:8]. It is this motive of action that engages my perfect agreement to submit to your proposal...and the sooner this is done both by you and me, with the strictest justice on both sides, the better. ... I am quite in earnest to have this request of yours, and this my own determination, pursued with steadiness and unreserved fidelity on both sides, and thus to have righteousness and peace firmly established.[35]

While the Countess labored to defend her case, Piercy countered with falsifications and diversions to strengthen his. Whether the dispute ended positively or not remains unknown since no further information is revealed in the correspondence. What can be said is that the further burden Piercy brought on did not dampen the Countess' resolve to establish her college. Her boldness could be seen in her solicitation of George Washington (1732-1799) for support of her project in February 1783. In her letter she stated that her paternal grandmother was related to him. She received a reply in August, and although George Washington said he could not be actively involved in the project, he did offer encouragement and his "general superintendence." More importantly, he expressed his high opinion of the Countess: for the privilege of possibly being related to her, for the wide respect commanded by her character, and for her "benevolent designs towards the Indian nations."[36]

Enclosed in another letter to George Washington in March 1784, the Countess included her address to "the Friends of Religion and Humanity in America" and described her extensive plan.[37] She understood that the undertaking needed to be handled

---

[35] Tyson, *Lady Huntingdon and Her Correspondence*, 231.
[36] Tyson, *Lady Huntingdon and Her Correspondence*, 231.
[37] Tyson, *Lady Huntingdon and Her Correspondence*, 232-234.

delicately and in stages. She intended to send clergymen, along with skilled workers, to settle in colonies, who would

> take pains to gain [the Indians'] esteem and affection ... Their duty will be ... to preach the glad tidings of salvation in the wilderness, to bring the inhabitants of those benighted regions form darkness to light, to the knowledge of the true God and of Jesus Christ.

Schools would be set up to teach the children "religion and virtue" and "useful knowledge," all "agreeably to that great principle of Christianity, love to God, universal charity and good will to all mankind." Close proximity between the missionaries and Indians would be necessary to stimulate natural and frequent conversation. A tract of land would be acquired for immigrant families, who could represent Protestants of all denominations, and who would be recommended by the Countess herself, "so that the settlers shall not be able to have bad people abroad among them."[38]

The method of execution sounded ideal, her commitment unmistakable; at the same time the conclusion of her letter showed that she ultimately surrendered the plan to the will of God:

> When we contemplate the revolution which Providence hath wrought in favour of the American States, that great work seems but a prelude to the completion of yet more gracious purposes of love to mankind. This idea fills the soul with joy and raises it to the most solemn devotion. Yet it is not for us frail mortals to determine in the counsels of the Most High. With humble submission to the Divine will, let us to our duty. Let us endeavor to spread his Name among the Heathen; let us endeavor to obey His Divine Precepts and to follow His gracious example of benignity to mankind. Unite with me then, my friends, in His glorious cause, you

---

[38] Tyson, *Lady Huntingdon and Her Correspondence*, 233.

The Bethesda Orphan House

who have seen and felt the mercy and goodness of the Almighty, who have been supported by Him in the days of trial and adversity and are at last delivered from bondage and raised to liberty and glory.[39]

In the end, the Countess' vision was never realized. Her death in 1791 prompted the Georgia Legislature to take possession of her properties.[40] The individuals she delegated to oversee the project had failed to save Bethesda—their determination could not avert Georgia's own interest for the estate, which was to convert it to a secular university. Following the war, the colony's efforts were directed towards developing commerce: nurturing religious life was not on the agenda. The hope that the Indians would one day receive the gospel, Lady Huntingdon wrote, "this thought makes me weep sweet tears of joy."[41] And while her vision did not materialize, we have much to learn from her perseverance. Through all of these struggles, she admitted that she was worn. Suffering from illness, she wrote in 1784, "looking on my tiring life of old age" she was "ready to faint under such as the prospect of so much labour." But she turned to Scripture for comfort and strength, specifically the example of Abraham in the fourth chapter of Romans: "These words revived me," she wrote, "Abraham *when as good as dead* staggered not."[42] Selina, rather than relying on her own ability, rested her faith in the promises of God.

---

[39] Tyson, *Lady Huntingdon and Her Correspondence*, 234.
[40] Harding, *Selina, Countess of Huntingdon*, 162.
[41] Tyson, *Lady Huntingdon and Her Correspondence*, 234.
[42] Tyson, *Lady Huntingdon and Her Correspondence*, 234.

14
A Painful Separation

The year 1782 the Countess of Huntingdon was to make one of the most difficult decisions of her life. While she was showing no signs of wanting to leave the Church of England, its representatives were imposing tremendous barriers to her evangelistic efforts. Appointing chaplains to preach in her home, setting up places of worship, establishing a college—all of these actions were intended to open up more opportunities for the spread of the gospel, in ways that the Establishment proved limiting. Decades passed with the Countess' work proceeding largely unchallenged. Chapels were raised up and operated within her rights as peeress, for they were *her* private chapels. Students were brought into her college and sent out to preach at these chapels, the majority of them unordained. The scope of her evangelistic work within the Methodist movement was expanding, in plain sight before the ecclesiastical establishment, and its leaders were looking on with displeasure. In their eyes, the Methodists posed a threat to religious order; but so long as these appointed ministers served under the umbrella of the Countess' protection, they could not intervene.

The Major Obstacle
But without ordination, these ministers faced limitations. A preacher unordained by the Church could not fully carry out his duties (such as administering Holy Communion), and so, without an official religious title, he could not secure a permanent position—which his living depended on.[1] Desperate, Methodist ministers, acquainted or unacquainted with the Countess, solicited

---
[1] Harding, *Selina, Countess of Huntingdon*, 172.

her help, hoping that someone in her position could make a more convincing plea to a bishop in granting them ordination. Her letters in defense of these ministers appear over a course of decades, and a sample of their tone shows the unyielding authority she was up against.

After Richard Elliot was turned down in 1752 for ordination, the Countess, though never having met the young minister, wrote to the Bishop of Exeter on his behalf. She received a prompt response, the bishop's words clearly revealing the intentions of those higher up to suppress the influence of the burgeoning Methodists in their midst:

> [I]f I may have leave freely to speak my sincere opinion, I conceive it a dangerous thing to introduce an Enthusiast into the Church and as a teacher. Mr. Elliot indeed tells me "that he is not sensible that any of his doctrines come under the denomination of Enthusiasm." All persons who pass under the Denomination of Methodists say the same. But as long as I am clearly convinced that Enthusiasm and tenets of a bad tendency are rooted in the sect I should act contrary to principle, and the trust reposed in one of my station, should I give them the least encouragement ... I must confess to your Ladyship that I have a tenderness for Mr. Elliot; nor excepting his late irregularities, do I at present know anything derogatory to his moral character. But I am still of the opinion that Enthusiasm will do less mischief out of the Church, than in it ... And my judgment would be the same were he my own brother.[2]

Evidently the charge of "irregularity" and "enthusiasm" was not an estimation of the minister's personal or moral character, but rather a disapproval of his failure to strictly observe the rules and orders of the Established Church. Itinerant preachers, for

---

[2] Tyson, *Lady Huntingdon and Her Correspondence*, 247.

A Painful Separation

example, were accused of violating parish boundaries. George Whitefield in 1756, preaching at Long Acre Chapel, received stern orders from the Bishop of Bangor: "I do hereby forbid you to preach any more at that Chapel, as you have no appointment from me, or license from the Bishop of London for that purpose ... if you continue to do you must expect to answer for this irregularity in a proper place."[3] That place was an ecclesiastical court, which Elliot and many other Methodist leaders were threatened to contend with should they continue their preaching.

Whitefield's defense before the bishop—the gospel: "I thought I might innocently preach the love of a crucified Redeemer and for his great namesake ... without giving any just offence to Jew or Gentile, much less to any Bishop or overseer of the Church of God." Convicted that he had committed no offense, he continued in his letter to the bishop:

> Controversy, my Lord, is what I abhor. ... As I have no design but to do good to precious souls, I promise to submit. But if your Lordship should judge it best to decline this method, and I should be called to answer for my conduct either before [an ecclesiastical court] or from the press, I trust the irregularity I am charged with will appear justifiable.[4]

Letter after letter the Countess wrote to bishops to no avail. To even be considered for ordination, required were testimonials signed by three clergymen, an adequate education (typically Oxford or Cambridge), and a thorough examination of the candidate's competency and held doctrine.[5] With many suspicious of the Methodists and the quality of education offered at Trevecca College, it was virtually impossible for a young candidate to fulfill

---

[3] Tyson, *Lady Huntingdon and Her Correspondence*, 249.
[4] Tyson, *Lady Huntingdon and Her Correspondence*, 249.
[5] Welch, *Spiritual Pilgrim*, 150; Harding, *Selina, Countess of Huntingdon*, 173-174.

the Church's conditions. It became obvious that oppression of the Methodists was blatant and all around: "Prejudices have hitherto run so high," Lady Huntingdon wrote in July 1776, "that few have been able to get ordained in the Church, though all preferring it and hopeless now of this."[6] Her distress over the situation was earlier apparent: "Thus far I have gone," she confided in Martin Madan in 1768, recognizing her own limitations, "but alas I can go no further ... May you stand by the cross of Christ in this humbling and trying instance."[7]

In spite of the obstacles, well into the next decade the Countess remained loyal to the Church of England, convicted that scripturally its "established principles" were "superior to any other," though she admitted that where the Establishment hindered her evangelism she was willing to break from its confinements.[8] John Berridge, however, admonished his friend concerning her "church-wall spirit," expressing in 1777 his judgment of the state of the Established Church:

> I regard neither high church, nor low church, nor any church, but the church of Christ, which is not built with hands, nor circumscribed within peculiar walls, nor confined to a singular denomination. I cordially approve the doctrine and liturgy of the Church of England, and have cause to bless God for a church-house to preach in, and a church revenue to live upon. And I could wish the gospel might not only be preached in all the British churches, but established therein by Christ's Spirit, as well as by national statute; but from the principles of the clergy, and the leading men in the nation, which are growing continually more unscriptural and licentious, I do fear our defense is departing, and the glory is removing from Israel. ... When I consider that the doctrines of grace are a common offence to

---

[6] Tyson, *Lady Huntingdon and Her Correspondence*, 256.
[7] Tyson, *Lady Huntingdon and Her Correspondence*, 250.
[8] Tyson, *Lady Huntingdon and Her Correspondence*, 256, July 23, 1776.

A Painful Separation

the clergy, and the Bible itself a fulsome nuisance to the great vulgar; that powerful efforts have been made to eject the gospel doctrines out of the Church; and the likelihood there is, from the nation's infidelity, of a future attempt succeeding; there is room to fear.[9]

Understanding Lady Huntingdon's loyalty helps us to better grasp why subsequent events brought her so much heartache. She was still hopeful about seeing the gospel break into the Establishment. In the same year, she wrote of her hopes in a letter to her chaplain Thomas Haweis:

> The Church door does and will stand open, consistent with order and legal appointment. Our gracious Lord has here also induced yourself and others to offer firmly the Gospel, and to that order that probably without this favor from Him never would have heard or thought about it.[10]

For this reason, Lady Huntingdon was determined to distinguish her work from that of the Dissenters. If there was to be any prospect of reform, she felt it was crucial to stay within the Establishment. And so under the weight of persecution, she pressed on, her "prayers and tears," she professed, flowing out of her "in secret."

The Chapel that Changed Everything

Then emerged the chapel that put under close scrutiny everything she had done until this point. Originally called the Pantheon, the recreational-turned place of worship became a point of controversy. An ancient Roman temple the source of its inspiration, the construction of this impressive, elegant dome in Clerkenwell, London was initially designed to offer public entertainment.

---

[9] Tyson, *Lady Huntingdon and Her Correspondence*, 259.
[10] Tyson, *Lady Huntingdon and Her Correspondence*, 257.

The Bold Evangelist

Corrupt practices forced a civil magistrate to close it down in 1776. Its availability for lease was brought to the attention of the Countess, who was no doubt drawn by its potential, but after consulting friends and assessing existing financial commitments, she passed it up.[11] The lease was eventually taken up by two Calvinistic Methodist clergymen, Herbert Jones and William Taylor, who transformed the desecrated site into a house of worship.

Opening as the Northampton Chapel in the summer of 1777, it was licensed under the Toleration Act as a Dissenting meeting house. Led by Jones and Taylor, whom the Countess described as "eminent and devoted ministers of Christ" and "faithful servants of the living God in heart, spirit, and life,"[12] residents and visitors of this booming suburb of London found the place a welcomed sanctuary in their midst. In a short time the numbers attending increased to thousands.[13] The building's grand architecture and beauty could only have facilitated the rich worship taking place there.

This was precisely what came to be the problem—at least to the vicar of the local parish church of St. James in Clerkenwell, William Sellon (1730-1790). While his regular salary was meager, his extra earnings from his congregation's voluntary contributions were substantial, so he was infuriated when his congregants left for the Northampton Chapel and took their contributions with them.[14] The thirsting souls that thronged the newly founded chapel lay bare the lack of spiritual care these congregants received from their former minister. His avarice was no secret and was most grossly exposed when he claimed his rights to the Northampton funds and insisted on his authority to preach at the chapel

---

[11] Cook, *Countess of Huntingdon*, 368.
[12] Tyson, *Lady Huntingdon and Her Correspondence*, 264.
[13] Turnbull, *Reviving the Heart*, 120.
[14] Welch, *Spiritual Pilgrim*, 153.

A Painful Separation

and appoint his own chaplains.[15] They were in *his* parish after all. Jones and Taylor refused to accept Sellon's terms.

Sellon took the case before the Bishop of London's ecclesiastical court, arguing that the two men were preaching illegally in his parish—they were Anglican clergymen conducting services in a Dissenting meeting house without the bishop's consent. The verdict came in: Jones and Taylor lost and they were ordered to discontinue services; so in the winter of 1779, the Northampton chapel was shut down, a congregation of thousands abruptly disbanded.

What did the Countess of Huntingdon do upon hearing of the results of the trial? As she had always been inclined to do: protect the cause of faithful ministers of Christ by using whatever means she could. In this case she once more leveraged her legal right as peeress, securing the lease of the Northampton Chapel and converting it to her own private one. A passageway was created to connect her house to the acquired building, and within a month, her residence opened as the Spa Fields Chapel. The implication? Any worshipper present was her guest.

To the bishop of London, the Countess tactfully defended her actions, avowing to "protect [the chapel] regularly under the Church," and by doing so prevent "thousands becoming Dissenters in consequence to it."[16] Cynical, almost scoffing in his letter, Sellon warned the Countess concerning the course she had chosen to take, slyly advising her to seek legal counsel.[17] The bishop's response was no more reassuring, though the Countess initially believed that the legal rights she had exercised for decades would still stand.[18] Thomas Wills (1740-1802), Cradock Glascott (1743-1831), Thomas Haweis—all Anglican clergymen—were Spa

---

[15] Cook, *Countess of Huntingdon*, 369.
[16] Tyson, *Lady Huntingdon and Her Correspondence*, 262.
[17] Tyson, *Lady Huntingdon and Her Correspondence*, 262, February 27, 1779.
[18] Cook, *Countess of Huntingdon*, 370-371.

Fields' appointed ministers and soon became victims of Sellon's litigious ends. Just like Jones and Taylor, they had no right to conduct services there without the bishop's consent. Their justification was that the Countess' personal property was not under the bishop's jurisdiction. Granted, Sellon's case against them had its merits: a place of worship that was housed in a colossal dome regularly seating thousands could hardly be considered a "private chapel." While the trial took place in the background, services at Spa Fields carried on; but in 1780 and 1781, Haweis and Glascott suffered the same end as Jones and Taylor.[19]

The Only Option: Secession

The silencing of these ministers left Lady Huntingdon with little option but to consider separating from the Church of England. "The persecutions are each hour arising against me," she wrote to a former student of Trevecca in 1780. "I am to be cast out of the Church [of England] now only for what I have been doing this forty years—speaking and living for Jesus Christ."[20] Sellon's victory was not only a judgment on Spa Fields but on all of her chapels—sooner or later they risked facing the same consequences. To prevent Sellon or anyone else from hindering her work, her only solution was to seek religious protection from the Toleration Act, as other Dissenters had.

The decision to secede was a complex and difficult one. Many who labored alongside her did not agree with her decision[21] (which was understandable given that the Countess herself had long been avoiding this situation). For this very reason, secession was all the more trying because she needed trusted clergymen to leave the Establishment with her: "I have asked none to go with me and none that does not come willingly to the help of the Lord and by

---

[19] Cook, *Countess of Huntingdon*, 375.
[20] Tyson, *Lady Huntingdon and Her Correspondence*, 265.
[21] Cook, *Countess of Huntingdon*, 377.

A Painful Separation

faith in the Son of God lay all at His feet; any others would do me no good and He only knows those best."[22] These words sprung from a heart that could not bear that any should suffer on her account unless they were fully convicted by the Lord's leading.

In the end, only two were willing to join the Countess: Thomas Wills and William Taylor. In their letter to the archbishops and bishops, these courageous men stressed that their decision was not out of a divisive spirit but from

> a simple view of glorifying God, of preaching the Gospel, and of being useful to our fellow-creatures, in that way which is most agreeable to our own consciences, and which we humbly conceive to be most calculated for the general good of those many thousands that attend the ministry of ourselves and those connected with us.[23]

In January 1782, the Countess seceded, which was how she came to form her own denomination, the *Countess of Huntingdon's Connexion*. Although most of her chapels were now officially considered Dissenting meeting houses, Selina identifying herself as a Dissenter did not carry the same sense as it did for others who dissented—for the latter were willing. Yet, at last, her chapels were free from the stern regulations that ecclesiastical authorities had been foisting on her for years; at last, the gospel message could be preached in her chapels without disruption.

Years earlier, sympathizing with Lady Huntingdon's discordant feelings about some of her Trevecca students flocking to Dissent, John Berridge offered powerful words on the matter, which most assuredly would have proven valuable during a time such as this:

---

[22] Tyson, *Lady Huntingdon and Her Correspondence*, 265.
[23] Tyson, *Lady Huntingdon and Her Correspondence*, 268.

The Bold Evangelist

> Some years ago, two of my lay-preachers deserted their ranks, and joined the dissenters. This threw me into a violent fit of the spleen, and set me a coughing and barking exceedingly; but when the phlegm was come up, and leisure allowed for calm thought, I did humbly conceive the Lord Jesus might be wiser than the old Vicar ... Be glad, therefore, my Lady, to promote the Lord's cause in any way, in your own line, if it may be; in another line, if it must be ... Dissenters may appear wrong to you, God hath his remnant among them, therefore lift not up your head against them for the Lord's sake; nor yet for consistency's sake, because your students are as real dissenting preachers as any in the land, unless a gown and band can make a clergyman.[24]

In 1779, before the Establishment pronounced their final judgment on the Countess' use of her peeress privileges, she, then seventy-two years old, ill, and weary from the hardship that appeared to loom ahead, sought comfort in knowing that she was bound to no earthly thing:

> As to my privileges, should either cruelty or oppression remove them, alas! How little loss to me. The few remaining days I have left might be most happily spent in obscurity with the faithful testimony of a conscience void of offence towards God and them. My wants are very very few, and being free from all men no loss can be sustained by me, and the poor and wretched offerings of my dregs of time can never be felt but as too little to that God, I willingly offer the loss of all things... the simple feelings of my heart resolving to trust the event in His hands who has hitherto never failed me in what shall be best for me.[25]

---

[24] Tyson, *Lady Huntingdon and Her Correspondence*, 260.
[25] Tyson, *Lady Huntingdon and Her Correspondence*, 265.

15
Lessons from the Life of Selina Hastings

Some three hundred years later, traces of the lifelong work of Selina Hastings can still be admired. The gothic-style Bath Chapel (of Selina's own design) survives today, currently a museum capturing the beauty of the city's historic architecture. At the Westminster College in Cambridge now resides one of the pioneering seminaries—Trevecca College. Alongside a quiet river in Savannah, Georgia, among rolling acres of majestic oak trees lies the legacy of George Whitefield's Bethesda orphanage. Continuing to gather in worship throughout England are churches in the *Countess of Huntingdon's Connexion*. Yet beyond the charming antiquity of a building or the fond remembrance of a bygone community, even more valuable are the lessons that can be gleaned from the life of this faithful woman of God.

We come to recognize that all followers of Christ are not without wounds in our past. But a painful past can and will be used by God for his divine purposes. While it may be a source of tears or resentment at times, it also has the capacity to fuel our passions and ambitions. Selina, witness to the awful consequences of greed that ravaged the bonds in her family, learned to do better with her own material possessions; victim of a disintegrated marriage, yearned to build a harmonious one for herself; distressed and alone in her childhood home, turned to prayer. Marred clay in the hands of a sovereign God can be remolded for His glory, for the work of His Kingdom (Jer. 18:4-6).

Selina's zeal for evangelism was unquestionable, but what can also be observed was the gradual progression of her movements. With each step she took, she became bolder for the cause of Christ—from evangelising one-on-one with workers on her estate, to opening up her drawing rooms for the aristocracy, to setting up places of worship all over England, to sending a mission team overseas. Selina was driven by a profound desire to spread the gospel: at each point in time, with the resources she had, she withheld nothing to carry out the urgent task. While most of us are no Countess, as sinners we bask in the riches of a most gracious and merciful Father, redeemed by the blood sacrifice of a loving Saviour on the Cross. It is this humbling truth that drives us to take that first step in proclaiming the gospel, and when we have done so, our divine call is to take another, as we surrender more and more of our lives to God (Rom. 12:1). In the words of Lady Huntingdon:

> Universal and constant usefulness for all is the important lesson, and when we are fully and wholly given up to the Lord I am sure soon the heart can long for nothing so much. At that time talents, life, soul and spirit may become upon earth a constant and living sacrifice ... that, is the one object of my poor heart.[1]

"Wherever a fellow creature existed, so far her prayers extended," Thomas Haweis shared upon the Countess' death.[2] When it came to evangelism, Selina cast a wide net, indiscriminate of who was a likely prospect for the gospel. Thus we witness the diverse people who benefitted from her ministry. Merely years after her conversion, she could write to Charles Wesley, "I have labored much among the unawakened: I let none pass by of any rank but I remind them of the fountain that is open for sin and for uncleanness."[3] Selina's genuine concern for the well-being and spiritual state of individuals from all spheres of life had far-reaching

---

[1] Tyson, *Lady Huntingdon and Her Correspondence*, 107, Letter to John Wesley, September 14, 1766.
[2] Tyson, *Lady Huntingdon and Her Correspondence*, 296.
[3] Tyson, *Lady Huntingdon and Her Correspondence*, 66, August 16, ca. 1743.

Lessons from the Life of Selina Hastings

results—such that the ordinary worker on her estate received her attention, the parent who could not afford to send her child to school, the minister soliciting help for a hospital or orphanage—even the aristocrat who remained unpersuaded by the Christian religion. Lord Chesterfield, for example, was nonetheless an instrument used by God when he opened up his own home for George Whitefield's preaching. Let us therefore not pass up opportunities that rise up all around us, not relying on our own human judgment, but trusting in the Almighty's power to use any soul for his grand purposes (Rom. 1:16; 9:21-22).

It is also amazing to consider the different backgrounds and personalities of those who converted during the Evangelical Revival—poor and rich, the ordinary citizen and the titled nobility, those inside the Established Church and those outside of it. Add to this the extraordinary reality that the key players in the Revival were converted at different times and locales, yet whose lives would in one way or another converge for the unified purpose of witnessing to the gospel. Occupying our little corners of the earth, each of us, wherever we are, whatever resources the good Lord has chosen to endow us with, plays no small part on this grand stage on which the Redemptive story takes place. We need the poetry of Charles Wesley, the self-discipline of John Wesley, the eloquence of George Whitefield, the endearing frankness of John Berridge, the humility of John Fletcher, and the audacity of Selina Hastings: guided by the Spirit of God, all of these individuals served together as one body for the glory of Christ (1 Cor. 12:4-11).

In a similar vein, as fallen creatures living in a fallen world in which believers have been redeemed, it is by God's grace that the foibles and failures of one believer are not those of the next, so that within the body of Christ brothers and sisters can lovingly carry one another with the singular goal of glorifying God:

The Bold Evangelist

> But God has so composed the body, giving greater honor to the part that lacked it, that there may be no division in the body, but that the members may have the same care for one another. If one member suffers, all suffer together; if one member is honored, all rejoice together (1 Cor. 12:14-26).

George Whitefield could set on fire the souls of thousands with his preaching, but he needed John Wesley and his aptitude for maintaining order and caring for new converts to do much good for the spread of Methodism in England. Whitefield himself had admitted to Wesley in 1740: "My business seems to be chiefly in planting; if God sends you to water, I praise his name." Likewise, the strong characters of John Wesley and Selina Hastings were in many ways offset by the conciliatory characters of George Whitefield and John Fletcher. As believers we must be sensitive to this unique makeup within the church and be mindful of the need for humility as we strive side by side for the advance of the gospel of Christ (Phil. 1:27).

Differing personalities and diverging doctrinal convictions inevitably exist among all servants of God and unity is possible because of our commitment to Christ (Eph. 2:19-22). It is this commitment that directs the watching world—skeptical, critical, cynical—to the God of love (Eph. 4:1-3; Matt. 5:16; 2 Cor. 5:20). We have seen how disputes among believers have resulted in unsightly offences, but even amid such darkness there lies the hope that the light of the Heavenly Father can break through. Christ, our supreme example of love and forgiveness, frees us to see one another in light of the Cross—enabling us to relinquish our pride and grievances. May our longing reflect that of the Countess: "O! May the Lord so unite us all in this everlasting bond of love and

Lessons from the Life of Selina Hastings

fellowship for His sake that as one heart we may follow His gracious and blessed voice through life and death to glory."[4]

We have witnessed the vulnerability of Selina following the deaths of her beloved husband and children. She took refuge in the promises of God; at the same time she was not impervious to heartache. Many of us can empathize with her instinct to withdraw when her wounds were still raw and stinging. Friends tenderly sought to comfort her, pointing her to the Christian hope in the heavenly glory. Yet a further compelling observation is that Selina's temporary absence from ministry was greatly felt by leaders in the Revival. These men wrote her letters not only of consolation but also of pleading for her to return to the ministry. As we consider our own service in the church, we ought to ask ourselves—have we sacrificed enough of our time and energy that a temporary absence would be deeply felt by our church family?

Selina's friends and all her warm interactions could not be thoroughly recounted in this short biography. Yet even glimpses reveal the importance of forming and nurturing friendships with brothers and sisters in Christ. Reading and understanding Scripture, grappling with difficult doctrine, facing conflict, persevering in ministry, drawing support in seasons of discouragement—Selina was deeply rooted in a Christian community that was a vital anchor in her journey as a believer. To her good friend Charles Wesley she expressed her gratitude for this spiritual intimacy and mutual concern within the family of Christ: "There is something at the bottom of old friendship in our Lord's family that is like Himself having loved His own, *He loves them to the end*; and as He cares over all our littleness so tenderly and lovingly, so do we to each other while our hearts are really kept with Him honestly and uprightly."[5]

---

[4] Tyson, *Lady Huntingdon and Her Correspondence*, 108, Letter to Charles Wesley, February 4, 1767.

[5] Tyson, *Lady Huntingdon and Her Correspondence*, 75.

The Bold Evangelist

Encountering the Countess' story, the accumulation of her life's work and her incredible vigor even in the face of complications and setbacks, may both fascinate and stupefy us. In her correspondence Lady Huntingdon confessed that her age slowed her down and her deteriorating health prevented her from throwing herself completely into her projects. Her determination sometimes hindered by exhaustion and exasperation, how then was Selina able to persevere? Only God could inspire and sustain such passion. Her blazing vision to bring the gospel to lost souls and her power to realize this vision emanated from her Creator. Reflecting on the gifts that God has instilled in each of us, we can be thankful that while we may physically tire from the work, we do not tire of the work itself, for our passion, our strength and our joy in carrying it out comes from him (1 Cor. 12:4-6; Phil. 3:12-15).

Finally, Selina had initiated countless evangelistic projects in a setting where the English Church was deeply set in its ways and citizens were unreceptive of what the Methodists aspired to do. Overshadowing the Countess' ventures was uncertainty. The project may have sparked excitement and enthusiasm, but who was even sure that it would succeed? Selina had the answer: "My grand maxim will support you," she wrote to Philip Doddridge in 1744, "Do that which is best, and leave the event to God."[6] Selina's surrendering of her labors to the will of God not only granted her the courage to enter into the unknown but also peace. This trust in divine providence was a recurring theme in her correspondence; over two decades later, she voiced similar thoughts to Charles Wesley:

> This we have nothing do with but to go on straight forward and not faint on our parts. The rest is in our Saviour's hands, who has all power in heaven and earth and there the government of all is. Let us, my dear friend, rest before Him

---

[6] Tyson, *Lady Huntingdon and Her Correspondence*, 71.

Lessons from the Life of Selina Hastings

in this and beg and expect every supply of grace and strength for what is before us ... Endure to the end through faith and prayer and to Him alone is our only care.[7]

And so by the end of Selina Hastings' long life she could make a declaration akin to that of the Apostle Paul in 2 Timothy 4:7: "My work is done. I have nothing to do but to go to my heavenly Father."

---

[7] Tyson, *Lady Huntingdon and Her Correspondence*, 108, February 4, 1767.

Acknowledgements

I would like to express my deepest gratitude to Dr. Michael Haykin for inviting me to write a biography on Selina Hastings, the Countess of Huntingdon. To be given the opportunity to pour my passion for writing into a meaningful project such as this one, at the same time raising young children, is joyful serving multiplied. I am deeply indebted to him for his encouragement and counsel along the way, especially his efforts in securing a publisher for the manuscript.

I would also like to extend my gratitude to Faith Cook for her meticulous and painstaking research detailed and narrated brilliantly in her 2001 biography *Selina Countess of Huntingdon*. She provided tremendous guidance regarding how to assess existing sources on Selina Hastings' life. Cook's voluminous work, along with archivist Edwin Welch's instructive 1995 biography *Spiritual Pilgrim: A Reassessment of the Life of the Countess of Huntingdon*, based on original manuscript papers and letters (which it has been emphasized were difficult to read due to Selina's illegible handwriting and lack of punctuation), facilitated the process of penning my own biography on the Countess.

I am extremely grateful to John R. Tyson, along with Boyd S. Schlenther, who collected, transcribed, and studied numerous letters of Lady Huntingdon, publishing in 2006 *In the Midst of Early Methodism: Lady Huntingdon and Her Correspondence*, a valuable "representative selection" of letters capturing her life and work. I was able to appreciate a smooth reading of the Countess' letters because of their editorial work, which sought to preserve accuracy but offer accessibility to the modern reader.

I would also like to extend my sincere thanks to the Editors Chance Faulkner and Corey M.K. Hughes at H&E Publishing for preparing the manuscript for publication. For the front cover of this book, special thanks to Marcos Rodrigues for his beautiful artwork of Selina Hastings and Paul Cox of Reftoons for the colourization.

Thanks should also go to my closest family and friends for their treasured words of encouragement. And the warmest gratitude to my husband Lee, who does so much for our household, enabling me to commit time to researching and writing, and who has never wavered in his loving support of my writing endeavours.

Priscilla Wong
Richmond Hill, Ontario
May 2021

About the Author

Priscilla Wong has a degree in English literature and French from York University and a Master of Theological Studies degree from Toronto Baptist Seminary. She also received a diploma in Radio and Television Broadcasting from Seneca College and a certificate in Creative Writing from the University of Toronto. Professionally, she has worked as an English tutor, technical writer, copywriter, and intern news reporter. Priscilla is the author of *Anne Steele and her Spiritual Vision: Seeing God in the Peaks, Valleys and Plateaus of Life* (Reformation Heritage Books, 2012). Her writing has appeared on The Gospel Coalition blog (Canadian edition) as well as in *Barnabas, The Gospel Witness,* and most recently H&E's *Strangers and Pilgrims on the Earth: Remembering the Mayflower Pilgrims, 1620-2020*. Priscilla lives in Richmond Hill, Ontario, with her husband Lee, and her three children Nathaniel, Jenuine, and Josiah. They are members of Sovereign Grace Church. At present she is balancing homeschooling with pursuing her passion for writing.

Suggested Further Reading

Selina Hastings

Cook, Faith. *Selina Countess of Huntingdon: Her Pivotal Role in the 18th Century Evangelical Awakening.* Edinburgh: The Banner of Truth Trust, 2001.

> *This highly-recommended biography offers an evangelical account of the life of Selina Hastings. The current biography is a preview to Cook's substantial chronicling of the Countess's life and interactions with numerous key figures in the revival.*

Davis, Mollie C. "The Countess of Huntingdon and Whitefield's Bethesda." *The Georgia Historical Quarterly* 56:1 (Spring 1972): 72–82.

Harding, Alan. *Selina, Countess of Huntingdon.* London: Epworth, 2007.

Tyson, John R. "Lady Huntingdon, Religion and Race." *Methodist History* 50:1 (October 2011).

Tyson, John R. "'A Poor, Vile Sinner': Lady Huntingdon's Vocabulary of Weakness and Deference." *Methodist History* 37:2 (January 1999).

Tyson, John R., and Boyd Stanley Schlenther. *In the Midst of Early Methodism: Lady Huntingdon and Her Correspondence.* Maryland: Scarecrow Press, 2006.

> *This book provides a valuable sample of Lady Huntingdon's correspondence, revealing the wide network she had with notable figures in the revival.*

Welch, Edwin. *Spiritual Pilgrim, A Reassessment of the Life of the Countess of Huntingdon*. Cardiff: University of Wales Press, 1995.

Background Reading

Coffey, John. "Evangelicals, Slavery & the Slave Trade: From Whitefield to Wilberforce." *ANVIL* 24:2 (2007): 97–116.

Dallimore, Arnold A. *George Whitefield: God's Anointed Servant in the Great Revival of the Eighteenth Century*. Illinois: Crossway, 1990.

Dowley, Tim. *Introduction to The History of Christianity*. Minneapolis: Fortress Press, 2002.

Houghton, S.M. *Sketches from Church History*. Edinburgh: The Banner of Truth Trust, 1980.

Noll, Mark. *The Rise of Evangelicalism: The Age of Edwards, Whitefield and the Wesleys*. Downers Grove: Inter-Varsity Press, 2003.

Turnbull, Richard. *Reviving the Heart: The Story of the 18th Century Revival*. Oxford: Lion Hudson, 2012.

Subject Index

America, xiii, 33, 42, 44, 52, 67, 80, 84, 94, 119, 124, 125, 131, 133, 134, 135
American Independence, xiii, 133
Anglicanism, 3, 10, 39, 40, 49, 50, 59, 70, 131, 145, 146
Antinomianism, 60, 113, 114
Arminianism, 67, 71, 99, 112, 113, 114, 115
Arminius, Jacob, 67
Arranged marriage, 18
Assurance of faith, 60, 65, 73, 113
Barnard, Thomas, 53
Bath Chapel, xiii, 93, 149
Baxter, Richard, 102
Benson, Joseph, 112, 113
Benson, Martin, 18, 49, 55, 87
Berridge, John, 9, 76, 77, 78, 90, 91, 92, 95, 101, 109, 142, 147, 151
Bethesda Orphan House, 119, 120
Bethesda orphanage, 149
Bible study, 53
Böhler, Peter, 43, 59
Bretby Hall Chapel, 92
Brighton Chapel, 90
Calvin, John, 67
Calvinism, 67, 68, 71, 80, 99, 112, 113, 115
Calvinistic Methodists, 84
Charles II, 8, 14

Christian Perfection, xii, 64
Christian Perfectionism, 66
Church of England, xiv, 7, 8, 10, 37, 40, 49, 56, 87, 88, 89, 97, 139, 142, 146
Confession, 53, 101
Cook, Joseph, 126
Cosson, John, 126, 127, 130
Cowper, Fanny, 63
Cowper, William, 94
Cromwell, Oliver, 8
Deism, 9
Devereux, Dorothy, 14
Devereux, Robert, 14
Dissenters, 8, 88, 121, 131, 132, 143, 145, 146, 148
Dixon, George, 98
Doddridge, Philip, 3, 57, 70, 93, 154
Eccles, Charles, 125, 126
Education, 37, 38, 97, 98, 105, 120, 136, 141
Edward III, 14
Edward IV, 14
Elliot, Richard, 140, 141
English Civil War, 8
Enlightenment, 9
Enthusiasts, 40, 98
Evangelical Revival, 2, 7, 9, 10, 19, 21, 31, 32, 38, 46, 49, 58, 68, 69, 71, 73, 83, 84, 87, 88, 100, 107, 109, 110, 151, 153, 162
Evangelism, xii, 68, 79, 84, 85, 87, 89, 142, 149, 150
Fanaticism, 53

Fasting, 40, 41, 60, 101
Fetter Lane Society, 43, 59
Finch, Selina, 14
Fletcher, John, 9, 76, 78, 83, 90, 91, 99, 100, 101, 102, 103, 112, 113, 114, 115, 116, 117, 118, 151, 152
Foundery, 61, 69, 81
Foundling Hospital, 37
Gambling, 36
George II, 17
Gill, John, 102
Gin epidemic, 49
Glascott, Cradock, 94, 145, 146
Glazebrook, James, 102
Glorious Revolution, 88
Great Ejection of 1662, 8
Grimshaw, William, 32
Gurnal, William, 102
Habersham, James, 130, 132, 133
Harris, Howell, xii, xiii, 10, 50, 59, 64, 66, 69, 76, 79, 99, 112, 119
Hastings, Elizabeth, xi, 17, 36, 37, 46, 47, 53, 54
Hastings, Ferdinando, xi, xii, 17, 25, 27, 73, 74
Hastings, George, xi, 17, 73, 74
Hastings, Henry, 76, 90
Hastings, Selina
  "A mother of Israel", 2
  as a mother, 4, 21, 27, 31, 74
  as a wife, 4, 21
  birth, 7, 13, 14
  childhood, 35
  conversion, 2, 13, 35, 36, 38, 39, 44, 53, 56, 64, 65, 73
  Countess of Huntingdon's Connexion, xiv, 2, 147, 149
  death of her daughter, 76, 92
  death of her husband, 75, 76
  death of her sons, 74, 76
  drawing rooms, 83, 150
  early life, 13, 16
  founding of Trevecca College, 95
  friendship with the Wesleys, 61, 62
  her chapels, xiii, 3, 32, 75, 89, 90, 91, 92, 93, 108, 146, 147
  her conversion, 150
  her death, 106, 137, 150
  ill health, 22, 45
  love for her students, 105, 128
  marriage, 16, 18, 24
  secession for the Church of England, 146
  temper, 3, 47
Hastings, Theophilus, xi, xii, 16, 17, 18, 21, 22, 23, 27, 29
Haweis, Thomas, 21, 35, 45, 89, 143, 146, 150
Henry, Matthew, 102
Higson, John, 98
Hill, Thomas, 126
Holiness, 60, 67, 113
Holy Club, 39, 110

Subject Index

Holy Spirit, 4, 10, 50, 64, 65, 69
Hotham, Gertrude, 82, 90
Hughes, Betty, 126, 130
Hume, David, 50
Hutton, James, 47
Hymn-singing, 52, 53, 94, 101, 121, 126
Indians, 42, 124, 128, 135, 136, 137
Ingham, Benjamin, xii, 9, 38, 39, 42, 43, 44, 49, 53, 54, 56, 59, 60, 110
Itinerant preaching, 10, 54, 67
James II, 14
Johnson, Samuel, 102
Jones, Herbert, 144, 145, 146
Keach, Benjamin, 102
Lady Betty. *See* Hastings, Elizabeth
Law, William, 41
Levinge, Mary, 15
Lord's Supper, 60, 88, 139
Luther, Martin, 7
Madan, Martin, 83, 90, 142
Margaret, Lady, xi, xii, 44, 45, 46, 47, 54
Means of grace, 60, 63
Methodism, 2, 10, 27, 29, 37, 39, 40, 49, 53, 54, 55, 56, 57, 59, 60, 66, 70, 83, 84, 87, 89, 92, 93, 97, 99, 100, 101, 111, 112, 113, 117, 139, 141, 144, 152, 161
Methodist movement, 10, 29, 40, 59, 83, 97, 99, 111, 112, 113, 117, 139

Minutes Controversy, xiii, 109, 110, 111, 112, 113, 114, 115, 116, 119
Molther, Philip Henry, 59
Moorfields Tabernacle, 69
Moralism, 9
Moravians, xii, 42, 43, 44, 47, 56, 59, 60, 64, 71
Mysticism, 79
Newton, John, 94, 123
Nonconformists, 8
Northampton Chapel, 144, 145
Oglethorpe, James, 42
Open-air preaching, 50, 52
Ote Hall Chapel, 91
Oxford University, 37, 39, 97
Persecution, 5, 8, 57, 143
Piercy, Richard, 126, 134
Piercy, William, 125, 126, 127, 128, 130, 131, 133, 134, 135
Prayer, 1, 10, 35, 40, 41, 44, 46, 52, 53, 60, 63, 83, 91, 98, 100, 101, 121, 126, 127, 149, 155
Predestination, xii, 66, 67
Princess Anne, 14
Productivity, 4
Protestants, 136
Puritans, 7, 8, 9
Rationalism, 9
Reformation, 7, 111
Religious freedom, 8
Religious liberty, 8
Restoration, 8, 14
Richards, Lewis, 126
Roberts, Daniel, 126
Romaine, William, 9, 77, 83, 90, 91, 92

Roman Catholicism, 7, 14
Rowland, Daniel, 101
Sanctification, 64
Scougal, Henry, 41
Sellon, William, 144, 145, 146
Shipman, Joseph, 106
Shirley, Frances, 82
Shirley, Henry, 13, 14
Shirley, Robert, 14, 15
Shirley, Walter, 94, 112, 115
Shirley, Washington, 14, 15, 16, 17, 18, 25
Sinlessness, 66
Slavery, 121, 122, 123, 124, 127, 162
Smallpox, xii, 49, 73
Society for Promoting Christian Knowledge, 37
Society for the Propagation of the Gospel, 37
Spa Fields Chapel, xiii, 145
Steele, Anne, 94
Stillness Controversy, 59
Taylor, William, 102, 144, 145, 146, 147
Tennent III, William, 125, 131, 132
Toleration Act, 88, 144, 146
Toplady, Augustus, 2, 75, 94
Townsend, Joseph, 102
Trevecca College, xiii, 79, 95, 97, 98, 99, 100, 101, 102, 103, 104, 105, 106, 107, 109, 111, 112, 113, 115, 116, 117, 118, 119, 124, 126, 127, 130, 141, 142, 146, 147, 149
Tuberculosis, 49
Tunbridge Wells Chapel, xiii, 94
Typhus, 49
Universal salvation, 68
Venn, Henry, 3, 83, 90
Wales, xiii, 10, 50, 52, 83, 99, 120, 124, 125, 132, 162
War, xiii, 133
Washington, Elizabeth, 14
Washington, George, 135
Watts, Isaac, 9, 93
Wesley, Charles, xii, 4, 9, 10, 38, 39, 42, 43, 45, 49, 59, 60, 61, 62, 64, 69, 77, 79, 83, 90, 93, 95, 101, 102, 110, 112, 116, 119, 120, 150, 151, 153, 154
Wesley, John, xi, xii, xiii, 2, 9, 10, 31, 38, 39, 42, 52, 53, 56, 59, 60, 64, 65, 67, 68, 69, 82, 84, 98, 103, 105, 109, 110, 112, 113, 114, 116, 119, 120, 122, 151, 152
Wheatley, Phillis, xiii, 124
White, William, 126
Whitefield, George, xi, xii, xiii, 2, 9, 10, 37, 38, 39, 40, 41, 42, 44, 49, 50, 51, 52, 53, 56, 59, 64, 65, 66, 67, 68, 69, 70, 79, 80, 81, 82, 84, 85, 87, 88, 92, 93, 94, 98, 100, 107, 110, 112, 113, 119, 120, 121, 122, 123, 124, 126, 128, 130, 131, 132, 133, 141, 149, 151, 152, 161, 162
Williams, William, 101
Wills, Thomas, 145, 147

Scripture Index

Old Testament

Isaiah
   43:19 90

Jeremiah
   18:4–6 149

New Testament

Luke
   19:8 135
Acts
   16:13–15 1
Romans
   1:16 151
   9:21–22 151
   12:1 150
1 Corinthians
   12:14–26 152
   12:4–11 151
   12:4–6 154
2 Corinthians
   5:20 152
Ephesians
   2:19–22 152
   4:1–3 152
Philippians
   1:27 152
   3:12–15 154
2 Timothy
   4:7 155

Date Completed	Name

www.ingramcontent.com/pod-product-compliance
Lightning Source LLC
Chambersburg PA
CBHW020906080526
44589CB00011B/470